Heather Brunskell-Evans is a social theorist and philosopher who specialises in ethics, medicine, sex and gender. After being an academic for nearly three decades, she now also works on national and international political projects driving the rights of women and girls. She is a spokeswoman for FiLiA, a feminist charity; a member of the management committee for OBJECT, a campaign group against the objectification of girls and women where she also contributes to research on surrogacy; and co-author of the Declaration on Women's Sex Based Rights. You can read more of her writing at www.heather-brunskell-evans.co.uk.

Other books by Heather Brunskell-Evans

Inventing Transgender Children and Young People
(2019, co-edited with Michele Moore)
Transgender Children and Young People
(2018, with Michele Moore)
The Sexualised Body and the Medical Authority of Pornography:
Performing Sexual Liberation (2016)
Reimagining Research for Reclaiming the Academy in Iraq:
Identities and Participation in Post-Conflict Enquiry
(2012, co-edited with Michele Moore)

Transgender Body Politics

Heather Brunskell-Evans

SPINIFEX

First published by Spinifex Press, 2020

Spinifex Press Pty Ltd
PO Box 5270, North Geelong, VIC 3215, Australia
PO Box 105, Mission Beach, QLD 4852, Australia

women@spinifexpress.com.au
www.spinifexpress.com.au

Edited by Renate Klein, Pauline Hopkins and Susan Hawthorne
Cover design by Deb Snibson, MAPG
Typesetting by Helen Christie, Blue Wren Books
Typeset in Utopia
Printed and bound by CPI Group (UK) Ltd, Croydon, CR0 4YY

A catalogue record for this
book is available from the
NATIONAL LIBRARY OF AUSTRALIA
National Library of Australia

ISBN: 9781925950229 (paperback)
ISBN: 9781925950236 (eBook)

For my young grandchildren Hugo, Hera and Octavia, in the hopes that their healthy bodies can be kept whole and safe throughout their childhood, free from the tyranny of 'gender identity'.

Contents

Contents

Prologue

I am often asked, "How did you get into researching and writing about transgenderism?" The answer is that I stumbled into it by accident. Five years ago, among my friends was a 'transwoman' called 'Emily'. Unlike many men following the current trend of no surgery, Emily had undergone surgical removal of his penis and testicles in order to transition. He narrated how, as a boy, he had been taught by his parents to 'make a man of himself' but couldn't help exhibiting traits which in the eyes of his parents made him 'not man enough'. As an adult, Emily had decided he needed to take on a stable, coherent, 'feminine' identity and had been prepared to do this through ingesting powerful chemicals, undergoing surgery (thereby forgoing future genital pleasure and any possibilities of fatherhood), fully understanding he had turned himself into a medical patient for life in a never-ending battle with his body. At the time, I saw his desire to identify as a woman as something which should elicit kindness, generosity and tolerance.

I don't think Emily really believes he *is* female, and certainly he knew that I didn't believe it but that I was happy to respect his fictional female identity. Why not? Gender norms are painful and disciplinary, and if for him 'femininity' is more comfortable than 'masculinity', then I supported his right, and anyone else's for that matter, to identify with socially constructed gender norms for the opposite sex.

Emily adopted many roles in my home — he came to parties presenting as a tall glamorous woman, but when brawn was needed, he jumped the 'gender ship' as it were. For example, at a house move, he whipped off his long blonde wig, revealing male pattern baldness, put on his jeans, and despite fifteen years or more of injecting oestrogen, he lifted heavy furniture as easily and as competently as the male members of my family. When I thought about Emily in feminist terms, I saw his identity as a woman as an indictment of masculinity. I believed that the implicit question posed to society by Emily and other 'transwomen' was: "What is a Man?"

My raised consciousness

A series of events in 2015 lifted a veil off a world of transgender ideology and politics with regard to 'transwomen' about which I had been completely unaware. I now know that that year was an iconic one for the trans rights movement, when the sustained political lobbying of the previous years reached an apotheosis (Burns, 2018).

At that time, I worked as a Senior Research Fellow at the University of Leicester in the Centre for Medical Humanities. Amongst other things, I researched, wrote and taught post-graduate students about the philosophy and social history of medicine, sex, and gender. One day, I walked past a newsagent shop and was struck by the cover of *Vanity Fair* magazine. Bruce Jenner, then a 65-year-old man, a one-time American athlete who won the gold medal for the decathlon at the Montreal Olympic Games in 1976, and father and grandfather of children in the (in)famous Kardashian family, had now apparently transformed himself into a woman named Caitlyn.

I wrote a short critical commentary on a University of Leicester internal publication platform called 'Think Pieces' (Brunskell-Evans, 2015). I described the photoshopped front cover image as bearing

> ... all the hallmarks of the sexualised performance of femininity: a state of semi-undress in a satin corset; long, tumbling hair; exposed 'look-at-me' breasts in a push-up bra; and a cinched waist to give an hour-glass figure.

I relayed further details: Jenner had undergone a 10-hour facial feminisation operation and breast augmentation although not genital surgery. I described how the online image was immediately followed by an explosive endorsement of it as 'iconic' by social and print media alike. We had also been directed to the appropriate moral stance. The simulacra of femininity were apparently accepted as indications of 'real' inner 'femininity.' We were given to understand that Caitlyn is a woman, a very brave woman, a woman who had not formerly been a man but had been female all 'her' life, including the time 'she' had fathered children. In an Orwellian twist, the artifice of gender (the constructions, fabrications and deceptions of Jenner's airbrushed and siliconed body) had apparently transitioned him into an authentic woman, but the empirical reality of his biological sex, including his fathering of children, was a fiction.

Strict parameters were laid down about how to think about Jenner. The media-monitoring USA organisation GLAAD (Gay and Lesbian Alliance Against Defamation, 2015) immediately issued a number of general guidelines directing us to what is good and what is bad with regard to what we should say. It told us:

> *DO* use female pronouns (she, her, hers) when referring to Caitlyn Jenner. *DO* avoid male pronouns and Caitlyn's prior name, even when referring to events in her past. *AVOID* the phrase 'born a man' when referring to Jenner. If it is necessary to describe what it means to be transgender, consider: While Caitlyn Jenner was designated male on her birth certificate, as a young child she knew that she was a girl. *DON'T* indulge in superficial critiques of a transgender person's femininity or masculinity. Commenting on how well a transgender person conforms to conventional standards of femininity or masculinity is reductive and insulting.

GLAAD posits transwomen have always been women: "Yes, even when they were 'fathering' children. Gender is what's inside — and for Caitlyn, finally on the outside too" (Gay and Lesbian Alliance Against Defamation, 2015).

Paris Lees, a British self-identified 'transwoman', warned that the majority of transgender people "face such hideous discrimination in the job market, not to mention social and familial rejection." Lees said that "many trans people are forced into sex work in order to pay for the medical aspects of gender transition, and often this puts them at risk of drug abuse and physical harm." Despite the privileged position Jenner occupies both materially and symbolically, Lees reminds us that Jenner "has endured years of hiding who she is, of trying to live up to other people's expectations of who she was supposed to be and, more recently, cruel tabloid speculation, ridicule and bullying." Lees points out that "Jenner matters culturally — and we need people who inhabit that space to complement the work being done at grassroots level to improve life for transpeople" (Lees, 2015).

In my piece I commented that on the one hand it is a cause of celebration that within a relatively short historical period, society is now sufficiently tolerant of gender confusion that a mainstream publication could support a man's 'gender identity' struggles. On the other hand, the claim that Jenner *is* a woman, rather than that he prefers to identify as a woman, had brought into focus the need to re-address the question, usually asked and answered by men: "What is a Woman?" I suggested that a catalyst for progressive social change could be to return to a feminist analysis of the social context — patriarchy — out of which Jenner's new 'gender identity' had emerged. I also commented that in liberal democratic society where free speech is lauded it was troubling that there seemed to be an authoritarian diktat of what one is 'allowed' to say regarding transgenderism.

It is hard now to credit my own lack of consciousness of the stakes involved in writing this article, but once written I can honestly say that I didn't even expect a response, let alone a backlash. Within 24 hours, Natascha Kennedy, an academic who identifies as a woman (and who also writes as Mark Hellen, see Kennedy and Hellen, 2010), demanded my University retract the article from publication. Kennedy complained it was

> ... in breach of the *Equality Act 2010* because it misgenders (i.e. deliberately uses the wrong gender) of Caitlyn Jenner. This is clearly not an unintentional misgendering but done for effect and done deliberately ... Misgendering trans people is abusive and likely to make trans students or employees feel threatened and is unacceptable. Under the legislation this represents direct discrimination and could be interpreted by students or staff as representing victimisation or harassment.

My 'Think Piece' was duly removed, sent to the University Legal Team, with all subsequent email correspondence copied to the Vice-Chancellor. I was extremely worried. Firstly, in all my years working in universities I had never been brought to the attention of a Vice-Chancellor. Secondly, the sheer fact that he was drawn into such a trivial issue demonstrated the nervousness and fear of everyone managing the situation. Thirdly, I had only a superficial knowledge of the *Equality Act 2010* and was rather frightened of being accused of breaching it. The lawyers responded:

> In our view the article is not discriminatory either directly or indirectly. It could be argued that in exploring the issues openly Heather is effectively advancing equality of opportunity through enabling people to understand better some issues relating to transgender.

The article was reinstated. I breathed a sigh of relief. I had experienced the whole episode as a form of masculinist coercive control of what I could think, and say, about being a woman whilst a man, Jenner, was given a global platform for that purpose. Sanity, or so I thought, had been restored to a world which I temporarily experienced as being turned upside down.

I remained preoccupied by the fact there clearly was a trans rights movement that had grown over a number of years and which was rather confident and self-righteous. How had I missed this development? Many people were obviously already 'in the know'. On the one hand, I received emails from numerous parts of the globe telling me how brave I was and that they didn't dare to speak out for fear of losing their jobs. I received another email from the heart of British Establishment, the BBC, offering a secret meeting. On the other hand, I received a letter from a mother saying my article was effectively telling her she was a bad mother for transitioning her primary school age 'daughter'.

I discussed this debacle with trusted colleagues. I explained that if women are compelled to accept that men who identify as women *are* women, both in law and in life, this could have a profound effect on women's previously hard-won human rights. One Australian colleague with whom I was collaborating on a project said: "Don't go down the transgender route Heather. It's a vortex — it will suck you in and you'll never get out. It will be the end of your career."

I was troubled. One day, some months later, a friend sat stricken at my kitchen table. Her daughter, whom I had known from birth, was now identifying as a boy. The school had been allowing 'him' to transition behind my friend's back, including using a male name and masculine pronouns. My friend asked my view on whether she should support her daughter's new identity, including her wearing of breast binders and her expressed wish for testosterone as soon as she reached sixteen and double mastectomy surgery at eighteen. I was horrified. My advice was that her duty as a mother was to refuse to go along with the trans narrative, and that she owed it to her daughter to continue to nurture and protect her body from harm. My friend told me that if she didn't affirm her daughter as a boy, it was she that would be seen as abusive rather than the school or those trans lobby groups responsible for the online propaganda her daughter was consuming. I knew something really serious was happening, not only to women and children, but also to the body politic. Trans identifying people make up less than 1% of the population but the effect on society was utterly disproportionate. From that moment I was impelled to act.

Chapter One
Women's Bodies

1.1 What Is a Woman?

An orthodox definition of woman distinguishes between biological sex and gender: Sex — whether one is male or female — is natural, biological and objectively factual. Gender refers to the social and cultural norms — and stereotypes — governing a particular sex category with regard to expected behaviour, role, appearance and so on. A gender critical feminist definition introduces the idea that hierarchical power structures gender stereotypes. Women are born female in the biological sense, but from childhood onwards girls have to navigate a series of social norms and figure out how to be 'feminine' and live as women. Similarly, men are born male in the biological sense, but from childhood onwards have to navigate a series of social norms and figure out how to be 'masculine' and live as men. Although gender constrains the flourishing and self-expression of both men and women, it is women in a patriarchy who experience the most egregious political, psychological and physical injuries.

This feminist perspective is termed 'gender critical' because, put simply, it requires us to bring a critical lens to gender. The norms of 'femininity' and 'masculinity' aren't free floating, imposed from nowhere and without ultimate purpose. They are motivated and have something to do with the sex-based oppression of women, and with the extraction of reproductive, domestic, sexual and emotional labour *from female people by male people*. Gender critical feminism is not a biologically-based identity politics, it is a *sex-class* based politics. Alongside inequality based on race, economic class and other markers, there is a distinctive form of inequality directed at women as such, by virtue of their belonging to the class of people sexed female and the social consequences that arise from this. Patriarchy is a historical structure that has oppressed women *on the basis* of their biology. To recognise the material basis of oppression does not make the oppression *necessary*: it makes it a political structure and thus open to challenge and to resistance.

Women with penises: Queer Theory

The ideas that underpin transgender ideology have emerged out of a specific philosophy — postmodernism and queer theory (a branch of postmodernism) — which rose to intellectual prominence in the 1990s and continues to be influential to this day. In particular, Judith Butler, a postmodern philosopher, challenges the gender critical distinction between sex and gender. Building on a theory of language developed by the postmodern French philosopher Jacques Derrida, Butler argues that the binaries of sex/gender and therefore female/male are language constructs which are no less oppressive than gender. As she sees it, sex is socially constructed all the way down — there is no material, non-social, immutable character to sex:

"the distinction between sex and gender turns out to be no distinction at all" (Butler, 1990, p. 11).

To buttress her claim that sex is not a biological fact but a social construction, Butler instrumentalises intersex people who, she alleges, confound the idea of binary sex and who "medical authorities have often mis-categorised and subjected to cruel forms of 'correction'" (Butler, 2019). She then seamlessly slips into the proposition that these medical authorities "play a crucial role" with *all* children "in deciding what sex an infant will be" (Butler, 2019, my emphasis). Since sex, according to Butler, is from the start normative, 'assigned' by powerful cultural authorities such as medical, familial, and legal institutions, those who develop non-normative identities without regard to sex take up a specific place as progressive radicals. With regard to transgender people, the deconstruction of sex

> ... opens toward a form of political freedom that would allow people to live with their 'given' or 'chosen' gender without discrimination and fear ... Those who fall outside the norm deserve to live in this world without fear, to love and to exist, and to seek to create a world more equitable and freer of violence (Butler, 2019).

Although the language we inherit orchestrates whatever existential decisions we make as individuals, nevertheless we all struggle to craft identities in a social context where conventions change and evolve. If we build on this existentialist account of social construction and the possibilities for freedom by deconstructing sex, Butler writes, "then one may be born a female, but become a man" (Butler, 2019).

"Transwomen *are* women: Get over it"

Stonewall, a UK publicly funded charity, describes itself as working to improve the lives of lesbian, gay, bisexual, transgender and queer people (LGBTQ) and is extremely influential in providing equality and diversity training for institutions such as the Equality and Human Rights Commission. Stonewall's definition of a 'transwoman' is someone who "is assigned male at birth but identifies and lives as a woman, and who may or may not have had surgery" (Stonewall, 2020). Lesbianism is now defined by Stonewall as "same gender attracted." Stonewall describes transgenderism as "an umbrella term" for those who self-identify as "transgender, transsexual, gender-queer, gender-fluid, non-binary, gender-variant, crossdresser, genderless, agender, nongender, third gender, bi-gender, trans man, trans woman, trans masculine, trans feminine and neutrois" (Stonewall, 2020). Anyone who disagrees with the assertion "transwomen *are* women" needs to just "get over it" (Stonewall, 2020a). Stonewall, through its incredible reach into institutions and employers (including schools and universities) explicitly advises, through their training programmes and propaganda — distributed via their near-ubiquitous Diversity Champions Scheme and their Top 100 Employers Index — that "transwoman are women" for all purposes (Stonewall, 2020). Further, Stonewall states that the officially accepted pathway to becoming a 'transwoman' should not be gatekept by any medical professionals whatsoever, but should be achieved through self-identification and an administrative procedure (Stonewall, 2018).

Yet the classification of trans according to Stonewall's own definition demonstrates that it can be a whole range of things. Does a man who cross-dresses on a Saturday, Monday and Tuesday become a woman on those days and thus require unfettered access to women-only spaces on the basis that denial would be a breach of 'her' human rights? The answer according to Stonewall's own criteria is yes. Similarly, Stonewall's definition of phobia extends beyond "the fear or dislike of someone based on the fact they are trans" (Stonewall, 2020). It describes *anyone* who does not believe someone *is* the other sex because of an "innate sense of their own gender, whether male, female or something else, which may or may not correspond to the sex assigned at birth" (Stonewall, 2020).

Any woman who cannot agree that an inner essential 'gender identity' is the unquestionable and irrefutable truth is now routinely turned upon by 'progressives' as a trans exclusionary radical feminist (TERF), no matter how moderate, thoughtful, or indeed trans friendly we are. Any equivocation other than immediate affirmation puts one out in the cold — one of Them, the Transphobes, Haters and Deniers, the Old Crones who want nothing more than to impede the queer revolutionaries who, through heroic pain and suffering, are dragging society onto the right side of history for the benefit of all our freedoms.

Making women's reproductive systems central to their identity is deemed by some transwomen to be exclusionary and therefore transphobic (see Bergdorf, 2018). A North American equivalent of Stonewall, The Human Rights Campaign Foundation, suggests the correct anatomical terminology to use in order to be inclusive of 'transwomen' is the term 'vagina' as a word only applicable to *men* (The Human Rights Campaign, 2020, my emphasis): "Front Hole ... internal genitals, sometimes referred to as a vagina. A front hole may self-lubricate, depending on age and hormones ... Strapless ... the genitals of trans women who have not had genital reconstruction (or 'bottom surgery'), sometimes referred to as a penis ... Vagina: the genitals of trans women who have had bottom surgery."

This new definition of what it means to be a woman performs a number of ideological functions. The category 'woman' is broken down into two sub-categories: 'cis-women', who are allegedly comfortable with the sex 'assigned' to them at birth; 'transwomen' who were wrongly 'assigned' male at birth but are in fact female 'inside'. It would be a mistake to think this new definition is connected to biological division: born females and born males who identify as females. If so, this would mean that 'transwomen' are simply males who (for whatever reason) prefer to identify with the socio-cultural gender role of women. In order to make the claim that 'transwomen' are *equally* female, it is necessary to erase biology in two ways: *Identity*, not genitalia, is the empirical basis of being female, thus rendering 'femininity' innate and not socially constructed and thus political. Binary sex is therefore not a fact but a social and political construct. This sub-division performs further political work, namely the creation of a hierarchy between 'cis-women' and 'transwomen': Although both sub-divisions are oppressed by patriarchy, 'cis-women' are privileged since 'transwomen' are doubly discriminated against because of transphobia.

The moral claims of those who insist 'transwomen' are women are founded on their idea that the human rights of 'cis-women' and 'transwomen' are not competing but fundamentally enmeshed.

Affirmative psychology:
A man is a woman if he says he is

Dr James Barrett is the Lead Psychiatrist at the adult Gender Identity Clinic (GIC) at the Tavistock and Portman Hospital National Health Service Trust, London. Barrett's approach to transgenderism is underwritten by queer theory and the deconstruction of dimorphic sex as an empirical reality. He argues that the claim that sex is dimorphic in mammals is "less than common sense." He uses the reproductive variations of *plants, molluscs, amphibians, reptiles, fish, and insects* to demonstrate his point that sexual reproduction has a large number of variations in practical application (Barrett, 2019, my emphasis). In contrast to sex, 'gender identity' is indisputable since how anyone feels is "their reality" (Barrett, 2019). "It is soul-crushing and miserable" for someone to live their lives inauthentically (Barrett, 2019). Transgender people, as a group, face disempowerment via stigma, discrimination, and bias. History demonstrates the blighted lives of gay and lesbian people who tried to live as if they were straight. Barrett believes that it is "equally soul-crushing to live in an inauthentic social gender role, and just as life-enhancing to, at last, be able to be one's true self" (Barrett, 2019).

In a spectacular move, it is now not only individual women or men who can't question transgender identity or speak about possible psychological causes for men identifying as women. It is now all psychological associations — professional bodies that register and govern practicing psychologists — that are compelled to comply with the fiction that trans identity, unlike all other identities, has no psychological basis or components. In 2017, a Memorandum of Understanding on Conversion Therapy (MoU) was ratified by all the major psychological service providers and therapy organisations in the UK, as well as Stonewall, NHS England and NHS Scotland. The Memorandum uses 'conversion therapy' as an umbrella term for an approach which would seek to convert or to help reconcile the person to their biological sex (MoU, 2017, no. 6). Organisations are referred to the latest British Psychological Society (BPS) guidelines on working with gender and sexually diverse clients to comply with equality and diversity issues (MoU, 2017, no. 17).

In 2019, the BPS also created guidelines for psychotherapists working with "gender, sexuality and relationship diversity." The committee was chaired by trans identifying Professor Christina Richards, who alongside Barrett is a lead consultant psychologist at the GIC. The guidelines apply to all those clients who are non-heteronormative, that is, they "do not identify as heterosexual, monogamous or cisgender" (BPS, 2019, p. 4). This group includes: lesbian, gay, bisexual and transgender (LGBT) people; people who engage in BDSM (bondage and discipline, dominance and submission, and sadomasochism); people who are agender (have no gender), are non-binary gender (have a gender other than male or female), are pansexual (have attraction irrespective of gender) and many others.

The BPS guidelines state that in the same way that current society no longer attempts to convert homosexuals to hetero-sexuality but understands "same-sex or gender attraction" as a normal part of human sexuality, similarly, "diverse gender identities are a normal part of human diversity" (BPS, 2019, p. 5). They point out that self-defined 'gender identity' is *not* in itself a mental health disorder — although exclusion, stigma and prejudice may precipitate mental health issues. Furthermore they argue that stigmatising trans individuals can lead to increased risk of emotional problems, suicide attempts and substance abuse. This should not be treated as *de facto* evidence that gender identities are psychopathological, since "it is the marginalisation and repression which causes the difficulties, rather than the identities and practices themselves" (BPS, 2019, p. 5). A 'transwoman' experiencing distress should have 'her' identity affirmed in therapy, and the grounds for counselling would be to facilitate 'her' "to live more comfortably, reduce distress and reach a greater degree of self-acceptance" (MoU, 2017, no. 6). BPS suggests that therapists need to be trained in the theories that underpin the affirmative approach such that they can work effectively with trans clients (MoU, 2017, no. 16).

1.2 Shaming Gender Critical Feminists

Intersectional feminism

In 1989, Kimberlé Crenshaw coined the term 'intersectional' to describe how interlocking systems of power combine, overlap and intersect with each other to affect women's experiences and opportunities. The term reminded feminism that women are not *one* homogenous category since our experiences are affected by different axes of oppression such as race, economic class, heteronormativity, ethnicity, age, religion and ableism. The 1980s had witnessed a wave of postmodern feminism that had become very individualistic and detached from analysing patriarchal social structures and power. Feminism was thus rendered toothless in defending its constituency — black, working class, disabled, lesbian women and so on — sometimes proudly announcing it was 'postfeminist'. Young women grew into adulthood thinking that feminist battles had been achieved, women and men now have equal opportunity, and that, for example, working in the pornography or prostitution industries is a feminist act.

The laudable analytical category 'intersectionality' has unintentionally fed into a form of 'feminism' that mobilises the new branch of the men's rights movement, transgenderism. Sally Hines, Professor of Sociology at the University of Sheffield, is a trans-affirmative intersectional feminist, who has reduced the term 'intersectional' to 'inclusivity' missing the point that including 'transwomen' in the category 'women' is not the same as white women including black women. She argues that questions around the position of "transwomen within feminism" cuts "to the heart" of "the constitution of 'woman'" (Hines, 2009, p. 155). She alleges gender critical feminists police the boundaries of who can or cannot be allowed into "the category of 'woman'" and, as such, hold rather unsophisticated, unreconstructed ideas that it is shared biology that constitutes the category woman (Hines, 2009, p. 157).

Hines returns to the catechism of queer theory which warns against seeing identity as "authentic." In deconstructing the "inside/outside binary" of who can be classified as belonging or not belonging to "woman," queer theory moves against the biological essentialism of gender critical feminism which excludes those 'transwomen' who "inhabit gender borderlands" (Hines, 2009, pp. 155, 156). In explaining "the marginalised histories, experiences and social and political demands of women," at the core of gender critical feminist politics is the concept "'woman' as a fixed category ... distinct from 'man'" (Hines, 2009, p. 157). She suggests that such feminist theory, for the most part, assumes that it is biological women who not only initiate "feminist interests and goals within discourse, but constitute the subject for whom political representation is pursued" (Hines, 2009, p. 157). Hines describes "feminist biologically based politics of gender" as nothing more than "identity politics" (Hines, 2009, p. 157).

Hines' analysis makes a number of reductive and frankly simplistic assumptions: firstly, gender critical feminism specifically *refutes* a direct link between biology and gender.

Indeed, as philosopher Dr Jane Clare Jones points out, it is gender critical feminism that offers "the radical proposition that what you like, what you wear and who you are should not be dictated by your chromosomes, hormones or any other marker of biological sex" (Jones, 2018). Binary sex is turned into binary gender, a political, externally imposed patriarchal hierarchy with two classes, occupying two value positions: male over female, man over woman, 'masculinity' over 'femininity'. Women are born as female in the biological sense, but from childhood onwards girls have to navigate a series of social norms and figure out how to be 'feminine' and live as women. Similarly, men are born male in the biological sense but from childhood onwards have to navigate a series of social norms and figure out how to be 'masculine' and live as men. There is nothing *authentic* about femininity: indeed women should *resist* it since femininity is the internalisation of oppressive gender norms.

Secondly, if Hines acknowledged that male and female are empirical biological realities belonging to two groups or classes invested by society with different social value, she would be forced to face 'the elephant in the room' of intersectionality, namely that human beings with penises belong to the class of person carrying out the oppression. As Jane Clare Jones points out correctly, "if you don't recognise that male and female people exist, there can be no male dominance, there can be no female oppression, there can, in short, be no patriarchy" (Jones, 2018). Thirdly, whilst castigating gender critical feminists for recognising that female biology matters when analysing power relationships, Jones argues that Hines endorses the very claims to an inherent, authentic, identity formulated by men who self-identify as women on the basis they possess "'the secret essence of womanhood'" (Jones, 2018).

When postmodern/queer theory was making its meteoric rise in the university in the 1980s and 1990s, I knew that the worst faux pas of which an aspiring academic in the humanities could be accused was 'biological essentialism.' It was alleged that using sex as an analytic category to theorise power reduces women to our sexed bodies. This is a claim that is now having a further incarnation: gender critical feminists are biological essentialists because they/we exclude men from the category of women, thus reducing 'transwomen' to their bodies. While intersectional feminists are ostensibly using the discourse of structural analysis (oppression/privilege etc.), in trans-speak, oppression is entirely individualised. Oppression is no longer a matter of structural material conditions, and how those material conditions are held in place by specific discursive practices. Oppression is now just a matter of some 'cis-women', namely bigots, TERFs, and transphobes, who have bad attitudes towards 'transwomen' (see Jones, 2018a). Instead of addressing men about their sex-based violence against women and men who identify as women, Hines lambasts gender critical feminism for actually *producing* rather than *critiquing* such harm. Gender critical feminists are accused of "a high level of antagonism towards transgender people" and of instigating "a feminist politics of hostility" (Hines, 2009, p. 153). Meanwhile transactivists' chilling threats of violence towards gender critical feminists go unremarked (see Chapter Three). In obscuring the material and sex-based nature of women's oppression, the men's rights movement and intersectional feminism work as one.

This *reductio ad absurdum* reasoning in academic inter-sectionality has now permeated popular culture. The journalist Zoe Williams, for example, reduces gender critical feminism to a form that believes "body parts define a woman," and that the "essence of womanhood" is communicated between "ovaries" (Williams, 2020). Williams asserts that the fundamental question for feminism should surely be "who has it worse?" (Williams, 2020). In a complete misunderstanding of its aims, she describes the *raison d'être* of the second wave women's movement of the 1970s as "taking the side of the oppressed." Urging women to do what we have always been taught — to put men before ourselves — she asks us to stand in that tradition and urges us to take "the side of compassion and fellowship ... in everything that made the women's movement meaningful and victorious: strength in numbers, solidarity and, ultimately, love." Solidarity is not exclusive: "it is compassionate and fights oppression ... That is why trans women are women, or womxn" (Williams, 2020).

In conclusion, intersectional feminism bolsters and re-inforces trans activism's efforts to undermine woman as a political category and class. The first thing that's really noticeable about the catechism of intersectionality, argues Jane Clare Jones, is how un-intersectional it is. Since sex does not exist, and woman is nothing to do with femaleness, then, unlike race or disability, for example, there is nothing meaningful about the axis of sex-based oppression. This kind of intersectionality holds a rigid set of views (pro-trans, pro-sex-work, anti-white feminism, anti-science) and a rigid point-scoring table which produces a hierarchy of who is allowed to speak and who must listen. Feminists who do not subscribe to the Faith are not only understood as hard-heartedly blocking the political advancement of 'transwomen' toward equal social status, but of wanting to completely erase their rights as human beings (Jones, 2018a).

1.3 A Woman Is an Adult Human Female

Women's bodies and binary sex

The queer line of reasoning for rejecting binary sex is false at every conceivable level (Wright and Hilton, 2020). Human beings, like all mammals, are sexually dimorphic. There are two distinct biological sexes that correspond with one of two distinct types of reproductive anatomy. There are only two kinds of sex cells — sperm and eggs — and no third type of sex cell exists in humans. At birth, more than 99.98% of reproductive anatomy is unambiguously male or female. Intersex individuals are extremely rare, and they are not a third sex. The empirical fact of the existence of intersex is not proof of either additional sexes beyond male and female or that sex is a 'spectrum' or a 'social construct.' Binary sex is an unassailable evidential fact — it is not culturally 'assigned': it is *observed* (Wright and Hilton, 2020).

Despite the empirical fact of dimorphic sex, Alison Phipps, Professor of Gender Studies at the University of Sussex, writes that the gender critical feminists' apparently "'reasonable' idea that there are two immutable biological sexes and that you cannot change from one to the other" is not only *unreasonable*, it is so dangerous it should not be discussed (Phipps, 2020, p. 10, my emphasis). She advises that those espousing such views should not be platformed and that feminist, LGBT, anti-racist and disability rights activists should refrain from "'civilised debate' about these ideas ... and call them the discredited and reactionary nonsense they are" (Phipps, 2020, p. 10).

This statement is staggering for a number of reasons: Not only does it deny scientific facts, but in brooking no dissent from the article of faith that binary sex is a social construct, it bears a fundamentalism and an authoritarianism that is shocking in a university. It is also a clarion call for the no-platforming of academics with a different view, depriving young students from exposure to a range of ideas, the history of knowledge, as well as to scientific facts. The importance of this dispute goes far beyond the local, internal wrangles of feminism: *the men's rights movement which needs to erase biological sex of any significance is mobilised by part of the feminist movement itself.* Any dissent is framed as illiberal, so that not only free speech but free *thought* is being erased.

Pregnancy and reproduction

Jane Clare Jones points out that the category 'woman' is "neither imposed nor chosen, discovered or assumed" (Jones, 2018).

Whether we like it or not, males and females are defined by our role in reproduction, irrespective of whether we fulfil that role. Our reproductive bodies have nothing to do with how comfortable we are with them and nothing to do with our personalities and who or what we like and dislike (Jones, 2018). To assert this is not to insist that because women can have babies all women *should* be mothers or *want* to be mothers. It is to argue that, from teenage years to menopause, every woman (barring medical conditions) has the capacity to have a child and, moreover, every woman is aware of the possibility of being involuntarily impregnated, not by an individual's identity, but by his penis.

Pregnant men

Pregnancy and birth are distinctly female acts since neither occur through 'gender identity' (Woman-Centered Midwifery, 2015). In a twist that would not long ago have been unimaginable, patriarchy is now mobilised through the flesh of women who, when designated as male, signify that men can become mothers too! In 2015, the Midwives Alliance of North America (MANA) issued a statement that the medical care of pregnancy and childbirth would now use the term 'pregnant people': the word woman is discriminatory against "trans, queer and non-gender conforming people" (MANA, 2015). MANA states that a number of points central to queer ideology are empirically true (MANA, 2015): Binary sex is not a "scientific fact" and "there is no benefit to women to hide this." The fact that sex is not a binary may be easier to see in other species, for example "*in butterflies*" (my emphasis). It is essential that birth attendants use inclusive language since without it, the overall physical and mental well-being of the birthing "person" decreases. In this way MANA claims that their ethical standards are humanitarian, helping relieve the oppression, violence and stigma trans and non-gender conforming people receive (MANA, 2015).

Sally Hines describes 'transmen' as having a civil right to parent (mother?) their own biological children. She is currently carrying out a publicly funded three-year research project on the physical, social and health care needs of pregnant 'transmen' (UK Research and Innovation, 2019). She says her research addresses some of the ways that queer theory has ignored the experiences of 'transmen' who desire to have their own biological child or who become pregnant by accident. Many 'transmen' retain their ovaries and uterus as well as the capacity to become pregnant either because they have chosen to socially transition without medical intervention or because they have only just begun testosterone treatment (or reduced it). The overall aim of the project is "to gain an in-depth understanding of the practices, experiences, and health care needs of the growing number of men who may seek to, or become, pregnant and give birth after gender transition" (UK Research and Innovation, 2019). Hines' project examines "how trans male narratives of pregnancy and birth bring new understandings to the embodied and gendered processes of parenting" (UK Research and Innovation, 2019). "Male pregnancy" shows that "social, technological and cultural transformations impact on how individuals live their gendered, bodily and intimate lives" (UK Research and Innovation, 2019).

Academic researchers into 'male' pregnancy argue that societal attitudes erect barriers to openly being pregnant and giving birth as a transgender (Hoffkling *et al*, 2017; Hines, 2019). Specific needs around conception, pregnancy, and newborn care may arise from "transphobia, exogenous testosterone exposure, or from having had (or desiring) gender-affirming surgery" (Hoffkling *et al*, 2017, p. 2). As a disenfranchised group, 'transmen' warrant attention to help them identify and address their particular needs that will involve them in a movement away from disempowerment to the expansion of their "ability to make strategic life choices, in a context where this ability was previously denied to them." In this context, "the very act of choosing to have children as a transgender man is an act of empowerment" (Hoffkling *et al*, 2017, p. 2). Men's maternity/ paternity raises larger questions about social justice and "citizenship parity for gender diverse people" (Hines, 2015). Public Health England is now committed to the health care needs of "being pregnant and male" and "ensuring pregnant trans men get equal quality care" (Public Health England, 2020).

Reclaiming biology

The neutralising of pregnancy as specifically female accommodates a tiny proportion of the female population — 'transmen' — who assert they *are* 'fathers'. In a gesture that intersectional feminism would regard as biologically essentialist, the organisation Woman-Centred Midwifery argues that erasure of the specificity that it is women who give birth contributes to "the cultural erasure of women's wisdom that the physiological power encoded in our female bodies is what creates, nourishes, and births live offspring and transmits culture" (Woman-Centered Midwifery, 2015). When women express their own experiences that their reproductive bodies have wisdom and power (perhaps rather obvious given the need for the continuation of the species), this is frowned upon by intersectional feminists as women *reducing* themselves to their bodies. Interestingly, intersectional feminists appear to acknowledge biology when the woman (wrongly) identifies herself as male.

Rivka Cymbalist, a doula birth attendant, worries that instead of supporting women, trans activists within the birthing world are concerned with language, and shout: "People give birth!" and "Chest-feeding is best!" (Cymbalist, 2020). This is a co-optation of the original aims to provide maternity care that respects the female body and its strengths. Midwives have worked hard to reclaim birthing practices from male-centred medicine. In the mid-twentieth century, women were given a deadening cocktail of drugs and were physically tied down, were subject to routine episiotomies, and had their babies pulled out by forceps. The work put in over the last 50 years to normalise woman-centred maternity is being jeopardised by a new movement to impose gender neutrality in the name of 'inclusivity'. In promoting the idea of birth as a 'neutral' act, patriarchal capitalism has been given the best form of control it could have wished for, namely control of the means of human reproduction through the control of women's bodies. The struggle against patriarchy must be led by those who own the means of reproduction: women. Cymbalist says that if we obfuscate reality by saying that, "actually, it's not only women who give birth," we lose our focus, and risk losing the small triumphs we have achieved in our struggle for woman-centred childbirth. Women have a right to bodily autonomy and to speak about their bodies and lives without the demand that we couch this self-expression in language which suits a patriarchal agenda (Cymbalist, 2020).

However, in the name of inclusion, the use of the word 'woman' or 'female' is increasingly avoided in organisations concerned with women's reproductive health. Planned Parenthood, the largest single provider of reproductive health services in the United States, now avoids the use of the word 'women' when referring to menstruation and supplants it with the term 'menstruators' (Murphy, 2016). Similarly, the UK campaign Bloody Good Period, which donates tampons and sanitary towels to asylum seekers, uses the word 'menstruators' rather than 'women' (Bloody Good Period, 2020). Cancer Research UK dropped the word 'woman' from its 2018 public health campaign against cervical cancer in an effort to be more inclusive of transgender people. The campaign urged "everyone aged 25–64 with a cervix" to go for a test (Bannerman, 2018). The UK government proposes the use of the term 'pregnant people' in place of pregnant women (Public Health England, 2020).

Many women object to the new language about our own bodies but are afraid to voice this concern publicly since it risks evoking the wrath of trans ideologues and their 'progressive' followers. Author J.K. Rowling (2020) writes that one of her objections to the evolving nomenclature is that

... the 'inclusive' language that calls female people 'menstruators' and 'people with vulvas' strikes many women as dehumanising and demeaning ... for those of us who've had degrading slurs spat at us by violent men, it's not neutral, it's hostile and alienating.

The 'backlash' to Rowling's intervention into the trans debate demonstrates the fury that can occur when women articulate the scale of male violence and insist their own bodily integrity and safety is a human right (see Chapter Three).

Gender neutrality

Transgenderism isn't an equal opportunities human rights movement. 'Transmen' do not question "What is a Man?" Men are not threatened by constructed males and so can afford to let some into the 'men's club'. Moreover, society agrees men shouldn't be asked to relinquish ownership of their bodies and sexual desires in the name of diversity and inclusion.

It is notable, for example, that Cancer Research UK only tests an 'inclusive' approach with regard to 'cervix holders'. Its campaign messages about prostate and testicular cancer address men, rather than "everyone with a prostate" or "everyone with testicles" (Ditum, 2018). While organisations in the women's sector have revised their language to avoid the word 'women', male-specific charities such as CALM (the Campaign Against Living Miserably) which is concerned with male suicide, continue to refer uncomplicatedly to men. While women's groups are aggressively picketed for being exclusionary, men's clubs are left unmolested (Ditum, 2018).

Transgenderism is the attempt to wrest female biology from women and in that process not only violates women's agency but our collective capacity for resistance. We need the language of sex difference if patriarchy is to be challenged and resisted. When discussing matters that affect women, the insistence on gender-neutral language makes it increasingly hard for women to articulate issues that arise from being embodied females. For example, how can women describe the maternity penalty as a factor in women's disadvantage in the workplace, without committing the 'essentialist *faux pas*' of associating women with pregnancy and motherhood (Ditum, 2018)? How can women point to the fact that men commit the vast majority of violent sexual crimes, including rape and child sexual abuse, and that many women and children have been the recipients of such violence, without the accusation that we are tarring innocent 'transwomen' with the same brush (Ditum, 2018)?

Far from loosening the shackles of gender, the institutional normalisation of transgender tightens them. The transgender social justice paradigm blurs the distinction between 'men' and 'woman' at a fundamental ontological level. For those of us who think we need the difference between men and women to describe our own experiences, to analyse how and why men oppress women so that we can actually resist oppression and bring about social justice, this is extremely problematic. The touchy feely intersectional feminism which supposedly is so 'inclusive' and 'kind' is more than just toothless in resisting patriarchy: it is another form of misogyny, aggressively helping to obfuscate and drown out, and even in some versions, to *actively* suppress, the very range of voices that make up feminism's constituency.

In the 1970s and 1980s, postmodern philosophy brought an original radical approach to the issue of identity and heteronormativity. It was not an individualist theory, but on the contrary, a way of understanding how 'identity', however deeply and personally experienced, was socially produced. In an appalling example of unintended consequences, over the following decades, postmodern theory and politics, particularly in the hands of queer theorists, has become an individualist, authoritarian self-absorbed fundamentalist theory and politics that beggars the original intention. What is blatantly signposted by the attempt to silence the terms 'female' and 'sex', and now 'vagina'— which as I have noted belongs unequivocally to the man in the new glossary of trans terms — is the urgent necessity to claim them.

Lesbianism:
Same-sex attraction or 'lesbians' with penises?

Sally Hines celebrates that transgenderism not only destabilises the otherwise easy divisions of men and women into distinct categories, but also that it destabilises the categories of straight and gay: transgender evokes "complex questions about the construction, deconstruction and ongoing reconstruction of ... sexual taxonomies" (Hines, 2009, p. 154). Trans people "destabilise the otherwise easy divisions of men and women into categories of straight and gay because they are both and/or neither" (Hines, 2009, p. 156). In the days before queer theory, homosexuality was largely understood as same-sex attraction, now deemed a hopelessly unsophisticated and retrograde definition which only makes sense when founded on clearly delineated distinctions between the sexes. Hines tells us that in her research, the narratives gathered from 'transwomen' who describe their sexual desire for 'other women' illustrates the limitations of this approach, since many are attracted to 'cis-women'.

A queer politics of inclusion aims to "dissolve the naturalisation and pathologisation of minority identities." Sally Hines argues that the impediment to this de-pathologisation arises not only from right-wing traditionalists but lesbian bigots who link 'woman' with biological 'sex' (Hines, 2009, p. 157). Not only do lesbians police the boundaries of who can be accepted into the category woman, they perform the double calumny of policing the lesbian community, excluding those whose identities fall outside of "that which is seen to be correct or fitting" (Hines, 2009, p. 157). As a result, 'transwomen lesbians' suffer rejection "as they attempt to define their gender and sexual identity and fit into lesbian and/or feminist spaces" (Hines, 2009, p. 155). In contrast, queer theory and politics do not focus on "who counts" as a lesbian but, in contrast, recognise and celebrate "sexual and gender diversity" (Hines, 2009, p. 157). Interestingly, Hines does not discuss whether she also castigates gay men for not sexually desiring 'transmen' with vaginas, nor does she tell us whether in her research 'transmen' experienced similar transphobic exclusions by gay men for not accepting their 'gentleman clits' as a male sexual organ, nor if they had any expectations to be seamlessly accepted into gay spaces.[1]

Lesbians are adult human females

A new organisation has been set up in the UK called the Lesbian, Gay and Bisexual (LGB) Alliance (LGB Alliance, 2020). Although the overall aim of the organisation is to advance the interests of LGB people whose rights are in danger because of the confusion between sex and gender, one of its particular aims is to amplify the voices of lesbians who experience additional discrimination. The eradication of sex means that lesbians, like all other women, have to accept that a 'transwoman' is a woman, whilst bearing an extra burden in having to comply with the idea that male genitals can be female. Lesbian women are now required, in the interests of inclusion, *not* to assert that the bodies they sexually or romantically desire are specifically female. In the alleged name of human rights, lesbians are told they are discriminatory and exclusionary not to desire 'lady dick'. Denying the reality of biological sex and supplanting same-sex attraction with same-gender attraction raises serious human rights issues for women. A substantial number of 'transwomen' retain male genitalia and clearly remain heterosexual men since many are still sexually

---

1 Susan Hawthorne in her book *In Defence of Separatism* (2019) counters this in a number of ways including in her discussion of the importance of lesbian feminism as a way of changing the structures of power in a patriarchy. She argues that this is "because it lies outside the institution of heterosexuality" and "it offers women an opportunity to go beyond the structures of 'patriarchal sexuality'" (Hawthorne, 2019, p. 72).

attracted to females. The injunction to comply, in the name of inclusion, with a man's sexual desire for her is experienced by many lesbians as a form of sexual abuse.

There has been strong opposition within the LGBT communities to the setting up of the LGB Alliance and a range of responses have been gathered: the aims of LGB Alliance are deemed objectionable, undermining the mission of the LGBT community, which is to fight stigma and discrimination. Any opinion other than uplifting one another, coming together, and supporting each other in the special community of LGBT is apparently regressive and hateful. Gender is not limited to body parts, and sexual attraction is much more complex and varied than what is dictated by your genitalia (Oldereide, 2020).

It always astounds me that men and women who rush to support women's rights to bodily autonomy when it comes to 'sex work' — pornography and prostitution — become very exercised when lesbian women want to retain their agency and same-sex attraction. Hines' claim that trans people destabilise the otherwise easy divisions of men and women into categories of straight and gay has very little intellectual clout with regard to challenging power. Lesbians are same-sex attracted women in a male-dominated society, and they exemplify exactly whose sexual freedoms are promoted by Hines' queer doctrine and whose sexuality is disciplined and controlled.

Patriarchy

Patriarchy is the cultural power structure in which male people are the default humans, and female people are defined by projections — and the acts of domination those projections impel and license — which flow from male people towards female people (Jones, 2018). But today, any human adult who says "I am a woman" must now be treated as if they were a biological woman, full stop. But 'transwomen' are not motivated to pursue the question: "What is a Man?" Men who identify as women do not challenge the men who police the boundaries of what is 'fitting' for 'masculine' behaviour; they challenge gender critical women, namely the very sympathetic women who are utterly tolerant of 'feminine' men. However, 'transwomen' are intensely preoccupied with the ancient patriarchal question: "What is a Woman?" Their answer is that a woman is who she says she is, so long as it is not actually a woman who says it! The queer redefinition of women to include men who identify as women has done little more than amplify the voices of humans with penises.

The gender critical activist, Posie Parker, has found a simple way to demonstrate the masculinist foundation of the transgender movement and the heated emotions that are aroused when women are non-compliant. She simply uses the Oxford dictionary definition of woman — 'woman: noun, adult human female' — and places it in public spaces using stickers and posters. This simple statement drives transgender ideologues and their supporters to apoplexy. In 2018, SKY News interviewed Parker and one of her detractors, Adrian Harrop, a medical doctor and activist (SKY News, 2018). Harrop had successfully campaigned for his local council in Liverpool to remove one of her posters, alleging that the definition is transphobic because the definition excludes 'transwomen'. When pressed about what a woman is Harrop replied, a woman "is any person who identifies as a woman" (SKY News, 2018).

Harrop accused Parker's actions as "demonising trans-women" and as making them "feel unsafe." He insisted her views have no place "in a modern, progressive society." In contrast, Parker alleged that Harrop and his "misogynistic allies" seek to erase women "in law and in life," and to "control what we think and what we say." To support her case, she gave the examples of changes in language advocated by trans activists calling women "menstruators" and "cervix holders." She claimed that men who identify as women define 'woman' on their own terms, and women, irony of ironies, are landed with having to fight to *include* themselves into their own category! At one point Parker asked Harrop whether, when working in Accident and Emergency, he would ask a patient's 'gender identity' before treating them in appropriate sex-specific ways. He responded: "Absolutely not, and you know that" (SKY News, 2018).

This short exchange encapsulates perfectly many of the contradictions and absurdities of transgender ideology. Harrop zealously supports the maxim 'transwomen' *are* women, yet, when pushed, reveals that even he doesn't *really* believe that 'transwomen' are biologically female, an article of faith he otherwise passionately espouses.

The now retired psychotherapist Dr Marcus Evans refuses to accede to the injunction by the British Psychological Society that he must not examine the possible aetiology of men's overarching determination to be included into the category of women. He argues that basic biological realities and differences between the sexes can provoke intense feelings of exclusion in some 'transwomen' (Evans, 2020). Some seem to believe that they have been traumatically excluded from their rightful place as women, and any attempt by women to exclude them is experienced as a psychological attack, as evidenced by their intense expressions of anger. Some 'transwomen's' sensitivity to exclusion extends to a belief that their psychological well-being, even their very human existence, hinges on their right to enter any female space whatsoever, even though women can feel this to be intrusive and threatening. Some 'transwomen' have a dogged insistence that their biologically male bodies offer them no competitive advantage in sports; or that their male bodies and sexual anatomy should not be seen as threatening to women in vulnerable spaces. Evans argues:

> Such delusions, in turn, have encouraged a sprawling academic ecosystem of self-described gender specialists who insist that the very idea of separating humanity into male and female — the basis of sexual reproduction, and therefore the survival of our species — somehow relies on an artificial construct.

Gender critical feminists have always insisted that the "most important space for women is their bodies" (Jeffreys, 2014, p.180). The historian Sheila Jeffreys points out that men's invasion and occupation of women's physical selves is the foundation of women's subordination. Historically, men have sold and swapped women as property in marriage and prostitution so that their bodies could be used for reproduction and sex. Jeffreys asserts that women's sustained attempt to wrest control of our bodies from individual men and from patriarchal laws and institutions has been the most important driver of feminist resistance since, without control of our bodies, women have no chance to access other forms of freedom (Jeffreys, 2014). It is our very biological body, in its political and social context, that gender critical feminism foregrounds in this latest twenty-first century battle of what it means to be a woman, and who has the authority to establish that meaning. The transgender social justice paradigm is currently colonising women's bodies, culture, politics and sexuality. The transgender definition that 'transwomen' are women, now endorsed by psychological services, promotes men's self-assumed authority to insist they are women, to speak on behalf of women, and to have a free pass into every area of life such that women can't articulate they are oppressed by men because the men are women just like them.

In conclusion, the moral argument that 'transwomen's' self-identity is a universal right and that it is interdependent with and indivisible from other human rights, reveals this assertion to be not only false but dangerous. Transgender politics oblige women to give up sex-based rights, while men remain untouched by the inclusion of women into their category. If 'transwomen' are differentiated from so-called 'cis-women' with regard to sex-segregated services such as hospital wards, prisons, domestic violence refuges, toilets and single-sex changing rooms, this is regarded not only tantamount to denying their rights as humans — 'Trans Rights are Human Rights' — but as an exclusionary denial of 'transwomen's' existence. The more 'the progressive Left' attaches itself to the transgender empire and compels women to faithfully adhere to their dictums, the greater the need for women to resist such authoritarianism and to continue their historical struggles for bodily, intellectual and political freedom. As the LGB Alliance states:

> A certain class of people experiences targeted abortion and infanticide; menstrual taboos; female genital mutilation (FGM); child marriage; high rates of domestic abuse, rape, sometimes as a weapon of war; restrictions on contraception and abortion; and a range of disadvantages in society, all related to their biological reality, not identity. There is a word for those people: females = girls and women (Oldereide 2020).

The denial of women's sex-specificity repeats in a newly invented format — the historic patriarchal refusal to grant specific recognition and value to women — to our rationality, bodies, and agency. The elimination of sex as a biological, material reality does not facilitate gender fluidity or break down gender hierarchy. On the contrary, it shores up the very patriarchal foundations which abuse women and children's human rights to agency and bodily integrity. Rather than transgenderism being about the opening up of gender for men to reject the norms of masculinity, it is the imposition of masculine dominance in a newly-minted form.

Chapter Two
Girls' Bodies

2.1 The 'Transboy'

The practice of medically 'transgendering' children has become normalised in North America, Western Europe, Australia, New Zealand and the United Kingdom. Although each country and cultural context has specific national Gender Identity Development Services, the rationale for medical transition is broadly shared. There have been three competing conceptual paradigms within which Gender Identity Development Services have operated historically — medical, developmental psychology and minority rights (Levine, 2020). Over the last few years, the transgender minority rights' paradigm has gained more traction and is now hegemonic in Gender Identity Development Services and successful in influencing public policy, the education of paediatricians, endocrinologists, and many mental health professionals. In this latter paradigm, any response other than affirmation of a girl's claim to 'be' a boy is understood as a violation of her human rights (Levine, 2020).

In this chapter, I examine the Gender Identity Development Service (GIDS) — the only publicly funded clinic in the UK — based within the Tavistock and Portman Hospital NHS Trust. The GIDS is mandated to

... provide specialist assessment, consultation and care, including psychological support and physical treatments, to children and young people to help reduce the distressing feelings of a mismatch between their natal (assigned) sex and their gender identity (NHS England, 2015).

The GIDS is also mandated to "recognize a wide diversity in sexual and gender identities [and] ... support children and young people to understand their gender identity" (NHS England, 2015).

Trans affirmative psychotherapy

Dr Bernadette Wren, Consultant Clinical Psychologist at the GIDS,[2] provides a clear rationale for the GIDS trans affirmative psychotherapeutic approach (Wren, 2014, 2020). She describes herself as a feminist "cis-gendered clinician" who has "come to value the postmodern turn in psychotherapy" (Wren, 2014, p. 272). She tells us postmodernism is a loose alliance of intellectual perspectives, but in particular she values Jacques Derrida (1967, 1973) and the queer theorist Judith Butler (1990, 2004) (see Chapter One).

The postmodern turn in psychotherapy at the GIDS specifically repudiates the psychodynamic clinical psychology or psychiatric approach for which the Tavistock is famous and is now fully committed to the trans affirmative model and its aims set out by the British Psychological Society (BPS, 2019; see also Chapter One). Postmodernism deconstructs the

---

2   Dr Bernadette Wren retired in 2020 as this book was being completed.

"fundamentalist modernist notions that underpin psychology," and in doing so, exposes "important social, political and ethical issues in psychotherapy" (Wren, 2014, p. 272). Firstly, the argument is that the psychodynamic approach wrongly assumes that the "self" is ultimately "knowable" and "coherent" (Wren, 2014, p. 273). Secondly, it belongs to "a scientific paradigm" for understanding human experience (Wren, 2014, p. 275). As such it is used to "... bolster the usual binaries in mental health: normal/abnormal, straight/perverse, healthy/sick" (Wren, 2014, p. 282). Thirdly, its model of childhood development "gives the power of definition and judgement too readily into the hands of the medical establishment keen to define and regulate gender" (Wren, 2014, p. 280).

The point of the affirmative therapy is not to help the 'transboy' find the causes for her masculine identity, for example, in developmental stages in 'his' life course that have gone awry. This would be to pathologise 'him' or to suggest that in some sense, in identifying as male, 'he' is misguided or delusional. The purpose of psychotherapy is to explore any experiences of conflict with, or distress regarding, gender identity, and to help the 'transboy' reach a greater degree of self-acceptance, but not to attempt to question 'his' identity in and of itself.

The World Professional Association for Transgender Health (WPATH) is the provider of guidelines (currently in their 7th revision) as well as continuing professional development courses for psychotherapists at the GIDS (and other Gender Identity Development Services in Europe, Australia and North America). Guidelines are produced by 'experts', namely the clinicians and academics who work in gender clinics and gender studies departments in universities, many of whom identify as transgender themselves. The guidelines provide unequivocally trans affirmative standards of care for health professionals working with transgender people. The GIDS adheres with complete confidence to WPATH guidelines despite the fact that WPATH is often criticised for its poor quality evidence base and its problematic practice of using clinical leaders to develop standards of care who are personally invested in the health care field (Van Meter, 2018). WPATH is also an advocacy group for the transgendered: it stipulates that health care provision is dependent on "not only good clinical care but also social and political climates that provide and ensure social tolerance, equality ... promoted through public policies and legal reforms ... that eliminate prejudice, discrimination, and stigma" (WPATH, 2011, pp. 1–2). Furthermore, WPATH is sponsored by numerous organisations, including The Open Society Foundations founded by George Soros, an issue to which I will return shortly.

A girl is a boy if she says she is

Bernadette Wren tells us it is difficult to convey "the ferocity and determination of otherwise rational and reflective young people to define themselves irreversibly with the help of powerful chemicals and, ultimately, surgery" (2014, p. 272). Nevertheless, the GIDS does not ascribe a *causal* account grounded in the 'transboy's' belief of being 'born in the wrong body'. That would be impossible from a postmodern perspective because the body and our experiences of it are *always* inscribed within language. Although the girl, for example, is fully committed to living as the 'boy' she 'knows' herself to be, Wren discounts "the seemingly direct experience of embodiment" (Wren, 2014, p. 279). However deeply held or experienced her conviction, her knowing is not "*evidential* knowing" since personal experience is "only one story amongst many with no privileged access to the Truth" (Wren, 2014, p. 279). The role of the psychotherapist is to eschew a biological explanation as a premature closure of the girl's creative possibilities for self-invention as masculine whilst also recognising "the integrity of many trans people's need for a settled sense of self with gender fixity as a pre-requisite" (Wren, 2014, p. 281).

Wren believes that all 'truths' we tell about ourselves are inevitably fictions to create cohesion within the 'self'. Thus the aim of the psychotherapist is "to enrich and develop" this gender identity narrative (Wren, 2014, p. 272). The masculine gender identity of an "assigned female" — the biological girl! — can be seen as "a creative compromise in endless negotiation with the self, others and culture" (Wren, 2014, p. 275). When a girl self-identifies as male, Wren believes this might be "a good enough compromise" of "her needs, historical conditions, and life circumstances" (Wren, 2014, p. 276). The role of the psychotherapist is not to search for a diagnosable condition, but to elaborate with the girl her *social identity* (my emphasis), namely how she is 'positioned' as a 'he' in relation to others, what that position permits her to be, and what narratives she is able to develop that are enriching and self-sustaining. Wren says that the aim of the psychotherapist is to "restore dignity to those whose transgender identification feels to them viable, respectable, and worthy of value" (Wren, 2014, p. 282).

Wren is at pains to separate the affirmative approach to the 'transboy' from a feminist gender critical approach. She argues, rightly, that this latter sees the girl's desire to 'fix' gender (through hormonal and surgical techniques) as "a perpetuation of sexist norms" (Wren, 2014, p. 281). She says such analyses deploy "seemingly foundational meta-narratives of the male/ female and hetero/homosexual binaries" and, in doing so, reproduce "regulatory power" (Wren, 2014, p. 273). She makes the same intersectional erroneous charge, namely that gender critical feminism "treats the anatomical differences between the sexes as determining psychological development ... and serves to marginalise women" (Wren 2014, p. 273). She wrongly claims that gender critical feminism believes in "'inborn' masculinity or femininity" and that in contrast, her form of feminism abandons such ideas and that it alone is attentive to "the potential oppression inherent in all gender roles" (Wren, 2014, p. 275).

The 'transboy' and 'his' body: Hormone therapy

It is a matter of grave concern for the safeguarding and protection of children (girls and boys) that the GIDS refers young people for medical intervention, despite a lack of evidence to support its stance, and that much of the data that exists points to the physical harms of the treatment and fails to support claims that medical transition is psychologically beneficial (e.g. Biggs, 2019; Brunskell-Evans, 2019a; Levine, 2020; Laidlaw, 2020; SEGM, 2020).

There are severe physical dangers of puberty blockers and cross-sex hormones: the drugs are unlicensed, their dangers to children's bodies are extreme, and without adequate trials (Biggs, 2019; Levine, 2020; Laidlaw, 2020; SEGM, 2020). Despite the GIDS' public assertions that puberty blockers are physically reversible so that if the young person stops taking them, their body will continue to develop as it was previously (GIDS, 2020), taking puberty blockers does not mean pressing a pause button so that children have time to reflect. It is more like pressing a fast forward button into cross-sex hormones and ultimately surgery. Puberty blockers and cross-sex hormones are the most controversial of medications known for risks to fertility, brain development, cardiovascular and bone health, plus impeding the development of sexual functioning, including for some never developing the capacity for orgasm, or experiencing pain in the uterus at the point of orgasm. One of the least discussed harms is the physical pain of orgasming that occurs after taking testosterone, and the number of women who eventually end up having to have hysterectomies and oophorectomies (removal of ovaries) (Dowling and Angel, 2019; Levine, 2020). Quickly, these drugs have become a political demand: campaigners and lobby groups have argued that to deny them to children is transphobic (SEGM, 2020).

The Trans Lobby's campaign for the 'human rights' of children to self-identify as the other sex and to receive body altering medical intervention is aided by "a cadre of elite billionaire philanthropists" (Bilek, 2020). Charities originally established to fight for homosexual rights (like Human Rights

Campaign in the United States and Stonewall in Britain) wield large budgets. The movement has accomplished in a few years what the movements for women's and for gay and lesbian rights took many decades to achieve. The journalist Jennifer Bilek exposes how three American billionaires have bankrolled the transgender movement on a global scale: Jennifer Pritzker, Jon Stryker, and George Soros (Bilek, 2018, 2018a). She exposes the relationship between these elites and the multi-million dollar medical-industrial complex in which they have stakes (Bilek, 2020, see also Chapter Four). In helping to construct medical-technological identities for children and young people, halting their puberty removes them from the very process that facilitates awareness of their own sexed bodies:

> ... unmooring children and young adults from their sex is a process of capitalist colonization of human biology for profit. Sex as identity opens markets and normalizes infringing on biological boundaries that constitute the very thing that makes us human (Bilek, 2020).

The majority of parents refer their daughters to the GIDS on the understanding that she will receive a diagnosis as to whether she *really is* a 'transboy'. If the specialist clinician decides that she is, she will be referred to an endocrinologist for corrective hormone treatment. There are numerous problems with this narrative. Firstly, there is nothing 'concrete' for the affirmative psychotherapist to find and then diagnose. No science can diagnose whether an identity is objectively 'true' since it is self-diagnosed by a girl whose body is completely healthy and phenotypically normal. Secondly, the hormone treatment will not change the sex of the girl: she remains forever female but will also become a medical patient for life. Thirdly, the girl's self-identity as male does not emerge from nowhere but is made culturally available to her, not only by Big Pharma and tech industries, but by her peers and an education system where LGBTQI inclusion and diversity policies in schools now teach children that human beings are not a sexually dimorphic species (Transgender Trend, 2020a).

One proposal often made by those worried about hormone therapy is to halt medical intervention until a clearer mandate is provided by up-to-date and reliable evidence of benign outcomes in adulthood. This is a perfectly understandable response, but one that approaches the problematic issue from *within* the postmodern model. What is at stake in safeguarding girls (and boys) is not lack of science or bad science — issues of course of the gravest importance — but a new so-called social justice paradigm which has made medical intervention on the bodies of healthy children even 'thinkable'. Also, the affirmative psychotherapists openly seek criteria from *outside* of a medical paradigm. When interviewed by the BBC, the Director of the GIDS, Dr Polly Carmichael, responded to a question about the harms of puberty blockers by prioritising the child's distress:

> But I think you have to weigh this up against the effects of not intervening. We are talking about young people whose sense of themselves does not match their physical body and the distress associated with that is often huge (Carmichael, 2020).

Carmichael warns that "we need to keep at the forefront of our minds that 'this continues to be a marginalised, stigmatised group'" (Carmichael, 2020). She says: "We're talking about *identity* here, their *identity*, and a feeling that their gender *identity* does not match that body" (Holt, 2020, my emphasis).

The 'transboy's' 'existential choice' to use hormone treatment

Dr Bernadette Wren asks: "How do we justify supporting trans youngsters to move towards treatment involving irreversible physical change when we ascribe to a highly tentative and provisional account of how we come to identify and live as gendered?" (Wren, 2014, p. 271). She enlightens us: the criteria don't arise from "narrow 'clinical' judgement" but rather from "broader social acceptance of the challenges brought by new medical technologies, new ideologies of self-determination and new models of parental responsiveness and love" (Wren, 2020, p. 40).

She elaborates: firstly, we now live in a social world where "medical intervention on and into the body becomes increasingly common-place" (Wren, 2020, p. 41). Medicine offers treatments that are conventionally accepted in many walks of life as ways of assisting our individual "identity projects." Wren suggests that the widespread use of technologies and pharmaceutical products (for example for contraception, abortion), as well as surgery, offer treatments that "can become formative of people's sense of self" (Wren, 2020, p. 41). Secondly, current childrearing practices afford children opportunities to exercise independent *existential choices,* including "considerable freedom to make their own mistakes" (Wren, 2020, p. 41).

Thirdly, many parents lovingly support their daughter in this "grave step" in order to alleviate her "pain and confusion" when her "gender feelings seem at variance with the sex assigned ... at birth." These parents, according to Wren, help facilitate for their daughters "the conditions for flourishing and rewarding lives" (Wren, 2020, p. 41). Wren gives a specific example, the mother of a 16-year-old called Sam who testifies to the clear benefits of her 'son's' "hormone treatments to masculinise the body and surgical intervention (top surgery)" (Wren, 2020, p. 40). Wren tells us the mother presents Sam "as a thoughtful and self-aware agent who knows what he [*sic*] needs to live in his [*sic*] body" (Wren, 2020, p. 40).

Although there is "a relative dearth of empirical research" to positively support medical transitioning, Wren informs us that "other issues are centrally at stake ... issues around power and rights, autonomy and authority, and responses to suffering — grappled with in our particular contemporary social context" (Wren, 2020, pp. 40, 42).

The predominant issue for the GIDS is "social justice" for the "gender diverse" (Wren, 2020, p. 42). Different orders of social justice are pre-figured by those who object to medical intervention, and those who support it. Objections to medical intervention *could* be seen as "socially just" — *or* they could be understood

> ... as a backlash against the expansion of gender norms and possibilities and the re-pathologisation of young people's feelings and desires — a regressive step after the decades in which the rights of sex and gender minorities have been advanced through legislation and social change (Wren, 2020, p. 42).

The transgender organisation Gendered Intelligence (2020) is influential on the GIDS' thinking and practice. The co-founder and CEO of Gendered Intelligence is Jay Stewart who was "assigned female at birth" but now "lives as a man" (Stewart, 2015). "Queer theory was the roadmap to my own self-understanding," declared Stewart (2018, p. 278). Stewart's advice is solicited in order to expand the GIDS' and other organisations' "understanding of the perspectives of trans communities" about working with "children who have trans, fluid, or uncertain gender identities" (Stewart, 2018, p. 47). Psychologists should not insist on the immutability of sex, since this effectively condemns girls to accept that they have no agency over their bodies. Indeed, Stewart suggests that we should now no longer think that girls and women have to accept their "bodily reality" (Stewart, 2018, p. 52). Girls should be made aware that there is nothing unalterable about the biological division between male or female and that they can transcend their female sex through wilful acts of their own 'self-choosing', "including surgery" if so desired (Stewart, 2018, p. 52).

The alleged 'neutrality' of the GIDS and Gendered Intelligence with regard to biological sex allows it to mobilise the power relationships that pin girls to their sex. The disavowal of binary sex has done nothing to destabilise masculinity. Rather it is a reiteration of the patriarchal claim that 'maleness' (agency, existentialism) *is* the definition of humanity, and girls can only claim these attributes in so far as they carry out an existentialist escape from their female sex with help from drugs and the medical establishment.

In conclusion, the transgender human rights framework that sanctions medical intervention is based on:

1. Refusal of the binary male/female which "prejudice young people's chance of having their experience of the body taken seriously as an intelligible identity, lived with dignity and integrity" (Wren, 2014, p. 282);

2. The belief that an inner male identity at odds with 'assigned sex' is not the product of individual, psychological and sociological reasons, since "transgender identities have been documented across many different societies and historical time"; and

3. "Nowadays, more and more people are challenging the rigid articulation of sex and gender prescribed by many cultures and voicing an incongruity with their biological sex" (Butler, Wren and Carmichael, 2019, p. 509).

The Tavistock, in which the GIDS is housed, is also avowedly and irrevocably tied to a large, global transgender emancipation health project. Under the leadership of its Chief Executive, Paul Jenkins, the Tavistock has tied its ethical flag to a particular mast of 'transgender' equality, diversity and inclusion. Members of staff are currently being guided through a pledge to declare that they are allies of the LGBT community. Once signed, each health care worker is then given a badge to signify they welcome members of this marginalised group, many of whom, it is alleged, are fearful of stigma and discrimination in health care settings.

2.2 A Girl Is a Young Human Female

After many years of passing under the radar of public scrutiny, numerous people (parents, gender critical clinical psychologists, academics, social workers) are now publicly voicing profound concerns about the exponential rise in the number of children and young people referred to the GIDS since 2015. In particular, there is great concern about the abrupt shift in the composition of those seeking treatment. Formerly, a significant majority of patients had been young boys. Now, two thirds of referrals are female, or what the GIDS describes as "assigned female at birth" (GIDS, 2020a).

Dr Polly Carmichael is repeatedly asked questions in the media about this phenomenon. She gives the same obfuscating replies: "We don't know," "It's complex," "We don't have all the answers," "We need more research" (Carmichael, 2020). Dr Elizabeth Van Horn, consultant psychiatrist at the GIDS, responded to a media question about the explosion in referrals of natal females by calmly remarking, "We do not know what might be driving this rise" (Van Horn, 2019).

However, behind the public 'face' of the GIDS there are many experienced clinical psychologists who disagree with the affirmative model and surreptitiously apply the psychological model of child and adolescent development with which they were trained. They have years of total immersion in the field of children's gender identity development and have generated their own hypotheses and answers to the exponential rise of girls presenting as boys. Yet none of their conclusions can be openly discussed. They have spoken behind the scenes to academics (Brunskell-Evans, 2019a; Brunskell-Evans and Moore, 2019) and latterly on public fora (Anonymous Clinicians, 2020). Shockingly, they cannot name themselves in case they are disciplined for advocating what is now called 'conversion therapy' or 'transphobia', and they fear for the security of their careers and livelihoods. They say: "There are elephants everywhere at the GIDS"; "affirmation of gender identity is really powerful, it is everywhere in the culture but we see it here undiluted"; "the total lack of evidence-base for anything we are doing, the lack of permission to use any kind of explanatory model for what we see ... so a formulation, or a hypothesis, we have no permission to make one" (Anonymous Clinicians 2018 in Brunskell-Evans, 2019a).

Sex/Gender

These gender critical clinical psychologists assert that the alleged inability to account for the increase in girls identifying as boys results from erasing the sex/gender binary as an analytical category. They want to retain the sex/gender binary: Gender is "the socially imposed expectations demanded of a girl by dint of her sex, meaning being born female" (Anonymous Clinicians, 2020). They say that "there are multiple, interweaving factors bearing down on girls as females such that the two discrete terms of sex and gender are related categories of experience which interact with one another" (Anonymous Clinicians, 2020).

Despite the current societal aspiration for gender equality, the culture is still highly sexualised. It signifies to girls that to be female is to be an object of male desire and male entitlement, and girls today are under ever more pressure to capitulate to the 'pinkification' and 'pornification' of culture. Lesbian girls who eschew feminine signifiers can often be lonely and isolated in their apparent idiosyncrasy, acutely aware that their same-sex attraction would be unacceptable to their family and friends. Dawning same-sex attraction occurs against a backdrop of homophobia, as well as a dearth of everyday, run-of-the-mill lesbian visibility. Autistic girls can find the idea of being 'transgender' helpful to make sense of their experiences of always feeling weird, not fitting in, struggling to understand social interactions and cues, being bullied, and feeling themselves to be outside the norm and 'girl' culture. The same is true for girls with eating disorders (see also Epilogue).

For some girls, the fear of leaving childhood behind, and the terror of becoming women, is overwhelming. The changes to their bodies during puberty, including the onset of menstruation, can bring about emotional turmoil. Their sexual feelings awaken amidst a culture of sexual predation where not only is there embarrassment, for example, in growing breasts, but fear that they will be pejoratively commented on and, worse, groped. For other girls, their bodies become the site onto which they can project their perceived failure to live up to society's expectations of femininity.

Teenage girls have long recruited their bodies as ways of expressing misery and self-hatred. Alighting on a trans identity can be "the ultimate act of *self*-harm hardly noticeable to many because it is so aligned with ... the ever-present attack on gender non-conforming women that exists throughout society" (Anonymous Clinicians, 2020). Gender non-conforming girls are just that — not conforming with rigid gender norms. In the past, they might, indeed, have been labelled 'tomboys', "but they were not taken to professionals for 'affirmation' of being wrongly 'assigned' a sex at birth" (Anonymous Clinicians, 2020.)

The GIDS transgender minority rights paradigm not only fails to safeguard girls' human rights to bodily autonomy and integrity but contributes to their disparagement. In ignoring the painful embodied experiences of girls which arise out of living in a highly sexualised and sexist culture, the affirmative model — and the possibilities it opens for medical intervention — leaves the normative cultural and psycho-social issues that bear down on girls largely intact and renders their bodies available for violation. Gender hierarchy is given fertile ground to flourish. The girl who has always felt different, isolated, confused by 'femininity' and whose tendency has been to dress, look and behave in ways which the adults around have designated as 'masculine', can easily conclude she would be a better boy than a girl, and from then on rigidly adhere to that belief. The GIDS affirms and compounds her distress about her female body, thus reproducing the very heteronormative power from which it allegedly releases her.

Clinical psychology

Gender critical clinical psychologists describe the limits of care that is offered at the GIDS because 'transgender' is the singular lens through which girls can make sense of their gender confusion. In the shift to a more automatic affirmation of children as 'transgender', consultations are now 'assessments' of their suitability for puberty blockers and hormone treatment and have often become extremely truncated at approximately three sessions.

In contrast to postmodern psychologists who see their role as affirming the girl in *being* a boy, gender critical clinical psychologists treat the girl's *wish* to be a boy as the phenomenon to be explored. In so doing, they advise bringing back 'into the mix' psychological and psychoanalytical concepts of identification, projection, unconscious symbol formation and so on that are now so roundly derided as pathologising by the affirmative model. They argue that the use of therapy to help the girl reconcile with her sexed body is mandatory since these girls exist within healthy bodies, regardless of how they feel about them, and it is unethical to intervene at the level of the physical body when this is not the problematic feature. The only way to alleviate dysmorphia is to explore their past and ongoing developmental processes in order to help them make sense of distressing feelings. These psychologists recommend an inquiring, trauma-informed psychological assessment with integrated therapy if needed. If this does not happen, children who have had very traumatic early experiences and early losses are being put on the medical pathway without having explored or addressed early adverse experiences.

There are multiple routes for girls *wishing* to be transgender. Girls who arrive at the GIDS belong to a heterogeneous group. They come with their own histories, personal circumstances, family dynamics and social contexts: the misery of sexual abuse and neglect; attachment difficulties, depression and anxiety; autism or other psychiatric co-morbidities; simply being lost, isolated, confused and miserable teenagers. An increasingly common characteristic of girls presenting with so-called gender dysphoria is previous online engagement with lobby groups and trans bloggers without any mediating influence or alternative explanation for their distress.

The social contagion identified by some clinical psychologists (Anonymous Clinicians, 2020) is confirmed by Dr Lisa Littman, Assistant Professor of the Practice of Behavioral and Social Sciences at Brown University, USA. In her 2018 research, Littman analysed data from parents who reported that their children seemed to experience a sudden or rapid onset of gender dysphoria (ROGD), appearing for the first time during puberty or even after its completion. Parents describe that the onset of gender dysphoria seemed to occur "in the context of belonging to a peer group where one, multiple, or even all of the friends have become gender dysphoric and transgender-identified during the same timeframe" (Littman, 2018, p. 1). These factors are not *external* to girls' identification as male but, alongside a sexist culture, they are important contributory factors to their self-construction as male.[3]

Muzzling dissent

The GIDS has attempted to hide the deep level of unease at the affirmative approach shared by some parents of children identifying as transgender as well as members of staff. The GIDS tells us that many parents lovingly support the 'transboy' to medically transition, thus painting a benign picture of parental love and approval. It often proclaims publicly that the decision for medical intervention is always a joint one between parents and children. The GIDS knows perfectly well that there are loving parents who do *not* agree that their children's emotional and psychological problems are addressed through affirmation of a 'trans identity' and who are deeply concerned their children are being fast-tracked without any serious psychological evaluation prior to medical intervention. In 2018, a group of parents met with Paul Jenkins, Chief Executive of the GIDS and Dr Sally Hodges, Children, Young Adults and Families Director. At this meeting the parents handed over a comprehensive research-based portfolio of evidence indicating and substantiating extensive patient safety failings for young people and families in the care of the GIDS (Brunskell-Evans and Moore, 2019, p. 6).

---

3   Journalist Abigail Shrier describes the alarming rise in girls being referred to or looking for gender clinics across the US as confirmation of Littman's findings. According to Shrier, "between 2016 and 2017, the number of gender surgeries for natal females in the US quadrupled" (Shrier, 2020, p. 26).

At the same time, Dr David Bell, a Tavistock governor and senior psychiatric consultant was approached by ten staff members (amounting to about one-fifth of the GIDS London-based service) who had grave ethical concerns similar to those expressed in the parents' letter — including inadequate clinical assessments, girls being pushed through for early medical interventions, and the GIDS' failure to stand up to pressure from trans lobby groups, in particular Mermaids, one of the main pressure groups in the UK which has been instrumental in enshrining the affirmative approach in NHS terms of reference for the GIDS (Brunskell-Evans, 2018, 2019a).[4] In 2018, Bell wrote a report, leaked to the *Sunday Times*, based upon the interviews and raising the Anonymous Clinicians' concerns while protecting their anonymity (in Gilligan, 2019). He cites the high percentage of children suffering gender dysphoria who also suffer from other complex problems left unaddressed, such as trauma, autism, a history of sexual abuse, eating disorders and so on. The letter says some children "... take up a trans identity as

---

4   Mermaids describes itself as "helping gender diverse kids, young people and families since 1995" (Mermaids, 2020). Its founder and CEO, Susie Green, took her 16-year-old son to Thailand to have his penis and testicles surgically removed, an operation illegal in the UK at that age, and subsequently illegal in Thailand for minors. Green has no expertise in child psychology or endocrinology but sees herself as qualified to contribute to clinical knowledge on the basis that she is the mother of a son who identifies as female. She has consistently and successfully lobbied for the idea that children can be 'born in the wrong body' (see Brunskell-Evans, 2018). She pushes for early medical intervention and relaxation of the age at which puberty blockers can be administered to minors. It is against the yardstick of Mermaids' position that Dr Carmichael can assert the GIDS' approach is moderate and proportionate (see also Chapter Four).

a solution to multiple problems such as historic child abuse in the family, bereavement ... homophobia and a very significant incidence of autism spectrum disorder after being coached online."

David Bell also comments that the true histories of these patients are of "highly disturbed or complex" children and are not properly explored by GIDS clinicians struggling with "huge and unmanageable caseloads" and who are afraid of being accused of transphobia if they questioned the "rehearsed" surface presentation of the children (in Gilligan, 2019). Bell concludes that "The GIDS service as it now functions [is] not fit for purpose and children's needs are being met in a woeful, inadequate manner and some will live with the damaging consequences" (Brunskell-Evans and Moore, 2019, p. 5).

Marcus Evans, a member of the Board of Governors who has subsequently resigned from his position because of the muzzling debacle, witnessed attempts by management to dismiss or undermine both David Bell's report and the letter from parents (Evans, 2020). This included accusing Bell of fictionalising the case studies he described, questioning his credentials, withholding his report from certain governors, and preventing him from attending a meeting to discuss the Medical Director's response to his report (Evans, 2020).

Perhaps emboldened by her ex-colleagues' utter frustration at the whitewashing of their concerns, Dr Kirsty Entwistle, a clinical psychologist and former employee at the GIDS' satellite clinic in Leeds, wrote about her hitherto unexpressed frustration in an excoriating open letter of complaint to Dr Polly

Carmichael (Entwistle, 2019). Among many other complaints she includes: The GIDS makes decisions that will have a major impact on children and young people's bodies and on their lives, potentially for the rest of their lives, without a robust evidence base; clinicians are afraid of raising their concerns for fear of being labelled transphobic by colleagues; the GIDS does not carry out a 'watchful waiting' approach, an assertion that only has substance when contrasted with lobby groups such as Mermaids which campaign for medical intervention *on demand.*

At the same time that Entwistle made her concerns public, and was urging transparency by Carmichael, in an extraordinary step, the GIDS threatened possible legal action against me and my colleague Professor Michele Moore as editors of the 2019 book *Inventing Transgender Children and Young People.* We had brought together in one volume, papers written by a mix of experienced clinicians and academics critical of an affirmative approach and the consequent lack of safeguarding of vulnerable children with multiple co-morbid psychological problems. An international law firm was employed by the GIDS which put forward claims about the following possible dangers of publication: "the book may contain comments which are defamatory of our client's clinicians and managers"; "patient confidentiality issues ... putting them at increased risk of unlawful discrimination and/or hate crimes"; "inappropriate conclusions drawn from incomplete data from ... the Early Intervention Study"; "many contributors ... will have been employed [by the GIDS] ... subject to confidentiality provisions

[that] may have been breached." The naïve demand was made of me and Michele Moore, as well as of the publishers, that we hand over the book before publication "to ensure the Book contributes to the debate in a fair, accurate and positive manner." If we didn't comply, then a vague and unspecified threat was made that "potential consequences may follow if you decline to cooperate with our client in a cooperative fashion."

The publishers initially got 'cold feet'. As editors we were confident that there was no legal case to be answered but we were simultaneously afraid that if the GIDS decided to throw the full financial weight of the NHS at us we could lose the very roofs over our heads in order to pay defence lawyers. Nevertheless, Michele and I remained determinedly non-compliant, eventually managing to persuade the publishers, previously blissfully unaware of the bullying tactics of trans affirmative organisations, that to allow ourselves to be driven by fear would contribute to the very harm to children and young people that the book attempts to highlight. One of the Trustees became as morally incensed as us, and the book was eventually published without any comeback whatsoever, either to ourselves or the publisher.

The GIDS is currently under scrutiny from certain sections of the media which are becoming more confident in challenging its practices. The extraordinary grip of powerful trans lobbies in silencing clinicians has meant that television producers and journalists who would like to expose the reservations of clinicians have found it difficult (Evans, 2020a). Clinicians speak to them in confidence but are afraid of publicly naming themselves (Evans, 2020a). Recently BBC Newsnight has produced two damning reports. The first describes the inadequate empirical evidence for, in 2011, lowering the age at which children can be administered puberty blockers in the UK from 16 years to the early onset of puberty (BBC Newsnight, 2019). This revised practice was rolled out through the GIDS Early Intervention Study mentioned earlier. BBC Newsnight reporter Deborah Cohen and producer Hannah Barnes based their investigation partly on research by Dr Michael Biggs, a sociologist at Oxford University. Biggs described how, between 2010 and 2014, puberty blockers were given to 50 children in the research study, yet this research yielded only one published scientific article on outcomes. The GIDS research showed no evidence for the effectiveness of puberty blockers: there was no statistically significant difference in psychosocial functioning between the group given blockers and the group given only psychological support. In addition, oral evidence was provided at a WPATH conference that after a year on the medication, children reported greater self-harm, and girls experienced more behavioural and emotional problems and expressed *greater* dissatisfaction with their body (Biggs, 2019, 2019a). Yet this very study has been used to justify implementing this drug regime to several hundred children aged under sixteen (Biggs, 2019, 2019a). Cohen and Barnes went on to write an article for the *British Medical Journal* about new allegations that the GIDS researchers might have broken rules when seeking ethical approval for the study and that they also misinterpreted another study's findings about potentially worrying effects of the drugs on changing bone density (Cohen and Barnes, 2019).

A second BBC Newsnight investigation revealed documentation that staff reported being discouraged from taking concerns about a child's welfare to the lead safeguarding officer, or referring cases to social services and seeking advice, and that this came from the Director herself, Dr Polly Carmichael (BBC Newsnight, 2020). We learned that the lead safeguarding officer could not comment as she *herself* had started legal proceedings against the Trust last year. The BBC Newsnight report revealed serious criticisms of individual staff members referring children to a medical pathway after inadequate assessment, in one case within the first hour of meeting with one member of the leadership team, Dr Sarah Davidson. Davidson is a proponent of queer theory and a proactive supporter of Gendered Intelligence whose work within schools she regards as a progressive contribution, alongside the GIDS, to a "multifactorial" approach in supporting "gender diverse children" (Davidson, 2019).

2.3 The Sacrificial 'Transboy'

Child 'consent' to medical treatment

The minority rights paradigm of the GIDS and other trans lobby groups such as Gendered Intelligence is founded on the idea that, with regard to gender, 'gender diverse' youngsters suffer the most oppression of all young people since they are stigmatised and vilified. In today's social climate, where all children are allowed a degree of freedom to make their own choices and the mistakes that can arise from that, they argue that 'trans youngsters' have the legal right to medical intervention on their own bodies, as long as they can fulfil Gillick competence criteria.[5]

The GIDS deploys three Gillick competence criteria to assess whether a child under sixteen can give informed consent. The first criterion is that the child has the mental capacity to fully understand the likely consequences, both positive and negative, of her decision-making. However, she (or he) is not psychologically competent to assess the likely consequences of a complex and contested medical area whose future ramifications will have little or no meaning. Not only are all the long-term impacts of hormone therapy unknown to clinicians themselves (Butler, De Graaf, Wren and Carmichael, 2018), a child will have little or no cognisance of a future in which she will become a medical patient for life, may come to regret lost sexuality and fertility (including, for example, the lack of breasts, ovaries and uterus), and the lack of organs for sexual pleasure. When a girl

---

5   The Gillick standard arose from the High Court's decision in Gillick v West Norfolk and Wisbech Area Health Authority [1985] 3 All ER 402 (HL), which is binding in the UK and approved in Australia, Canada, and New Zealand. In this landmark case, Mrs Gillick, a mother of 10, took the West Norfolk and Wisbech Health Authority to court for issuing a circular advising doctors on providing contraception to minors (here, under age 16), which the Authority left up to the doctor's discretion. Mrs Gillick argued that parental rights trumped consent where the child in question was under age 16. The court responded by saying that parental rights do not exist; <https://medical-dictionary.thefreedictionary.com/Gillick+competence>

is provided with hormone therapy, the issue is not a neutral act, or an issue to be decided on a case-by-case basis founded on whether the child has the capacity to consent defined by Gillick competence: "It is simply not possible for a child or adolescent to conceptualise a loss of fertility or sexual pleasure before they have developed their adult body" (Anonymous Clinicians, 2020).

Moreover, the information given by the GIDS to children is not factual. For example, children are told that hormone blockers will make them feel less worried about growing up in 'the wrong body' and will give them more time and space to reflect. This reassurance is contradicted by GIDS' own research evidence collected from the Early Intervention Study (described above) which demonstrates that after one year, young people report an increase in body dissatisfaction. Put differently, rather than giving them the opportunity to change their minds, children almost invariably proceed to cross-sex hormones (Endocrine Society, 2017).

The second criterion is that the child has been advised of *alternative* treatments (including no treatment at all), and the likely positive and negative consequences of those alternatives. However, the GIDS uniformly directs parents and children to resources and information given by Gendered Intelligence and Mermaids, pressure groups which have no training in child psychology yet have effectively lobbied for the past 30 years for the unequivocal adoption of an affirmative model and the normalisation and desirability of hormone therapy. There *is* an alternative model, most notably a gender critical model but the GIDS does not direct parents and children towards it. This model has many ethical and epistemic advantages over the gender affirmative model. It is not based on tentative, unverifiable and disputed neuro-scientific claims that the natal brain is sexed and that a natal male brain can somehow find itself in a female baby. It is based on unassailable evidence that gender is socially produced, a fact evidenced by historically and culturally different social norms and mores for girls and boys, women and men. The gender critical model does not confine girls (and boys) to gender stereotypes but supports them to be comfortable in their own bodies, and helps avoid a lifetime of medical intervention with life-long deleterious consequences which cannot, despite the young person's fantasy, ultimately transform their body to the opposite sex.

The third criterion is that the child has not been influenced by others in its decision-making. This is an impossible criterion to fulfil. Children are social beings as well as independent actors who 'take up' normative identities made available to them within the prevalent sexist culture — as well as from their peers — which may lead them to wish for, and consent to, harmful treatments. The presently circulating cultural notion that some children are 'innately' the opposite sex and can transition to it physically means that many young people are unlikely to be held back by any concerned GIDS clinician who prefers a psycho-therapeutic approach.

However, Gendered Intelligence objects to the proposition that hormone treatment is unlawful or unethical since children cannot, by reference to Gillick criteria, validly give consent. As they argue:

Since other children of sixteen years and under, if considered Gillick competent, are deemed fit to consent to life-saving medical intervention, it follows that transgender children if not accorded this right, are being discriminated against (Gendered Intelligence, 2020a).

In suggesting that medical intervention is 'life-saving', Stewart, as the CEO, uses the term 'gender dysphoria'— an allegedly pathologising term that Gendered Intelligence has dedicated itself to reject. Using the term in this context allows Stewart to firstly describe gender dysphoria as a medical condition and thus one that necessitates a medical solution, and secondly to call upon the manipulative myth, first promulgated by Stonewall and now reproduced by all pro-trans lobby groups and popularly accepted as factually true, that unless children are affirmed as 'trans', and receive the requisite medical treatment, they will commit suicide.[6] They request that in order to prevent such appalling consequences if children's wishes are not immediately conceded, the 'gate-keeping' adult must relinquish the authority to make the decision on behalf of the child and hand it to the child. "These young people know themselves, know their bodies and know what is right for them individually"

---

6   The common language used by trans affirmative organisations and some of the parents they represent is the following: "I want a happy daughter, not a dead son." "We prefer to have a living son than a dead daughter." "Do you want a happy little girl or a dead little boy?" "My wife and I decided that we would much rather have a happy, healthy daughter than a dead son." For an analysis of research evidence about inflated suicide statistics and the political purposes to which they are put, see Biggs (2018, 2018a), 4thWaveNow (2015), Anonymous Scientist (2016) and Transgender Trend (2019).

(Gendered Intelligence, 2020a). Stewart minimises the physical cost to the body if the child turns out to regret the decision by comparing hormone intervention to other irreversible physical transformations such as "tattoos and giving birth" (Stewart, 2018, p. 52). He argues that in many areas of life, we leave children with a margin of error to make their own mistakes. The reason why society is specifically preoccupied with irreversible medical treatments is "because there is an undercurrent in our societal thinking that being trans is *wrong*" (Stewart, 2018, p. 52).

The framework of criteria for assessing informed consent deployed by the GIDS and Gendered Intelligence is not an overall consideration of the ethics of hormone intervention but a superficial model for correct procedure. Given the disputed 'truths' about the aetiology of transgenderism, the experimental nature of the treatment, the significance of the intervention, and the potential irreversibility of the consequences, as well as the girl's emotional and psychological immaturity, she cannot be deemed capable of properly informed consent. The ethical issue of whether the girl under sixteen years of age can consent to medical transition to become a 'boy' goes far beyond Gillick competence since a girl's capacity for consent is not sufficient to counter systemic sexist attitudes and beliefs.

Sheila Jeffreys (2014) describes the effects of the drug treatment and sexual surgeries as a breach of girls' and young women's reproductive rights, as well as causing harm to their bodily integrity and future health. The transgendering of children can "be seen as a particularly harmful form of ... abuse" (Jeffreys, 2014, p. 138). She reflects on the future consequences of the popularisation of medically 'transgendering' girls and predicts "the distress they are likely to suffer when they change their minds" (Jeffreys, 2014, p. 139).

Marcus Evans points out that there is considerable evidence that children are consenting at the GIDS to treatments with long-term implications, with very little real understanding of the consequences for their future adult lives (Evans, 2020a). Children of twelve and under are not really aware of what it will mean to become an infertile adult, who cannot have an orgasm and has to remain a patient dependent on hormones and medical care for the rest of their lives. Girls cannot know what it will mean in the future to have to undergo "hysterectomy to avoid vaginal atrophy" (Evans, 2020a, p. 3). He describes the 'affirmative approach' as risking sending children down a path towards concrete and sometimes irreversible medical interventions for what is in very many cases a psychological problem. He argues this approach is "driven by political ideology rather than clinical need" (Evans, 2020a, p. 1). The 'affirmation approach' ignores "the complex relationship between the overt symptomatic picture and trauma, social anxieties and even the relatively normal turbulence of adolescence" (Evans, 2020a, p. 1).

The iatrogenic 'transboy'

Girls are always referred to by the GIDS in gender neutral terms: 'gender variant', 'trans youngsters', 'young trans people', 'transgendered youth'. When pressed by the media about the exponential rise of 'trans youth' now seeking to medical transition, Dr Polly Carmichael's stock answer is that this is positive, that it is the consequence of reduced social stigma, increased access to services as well as "increased awareness of the possibilities around physical treatments for younger adolescents" (Carmichael, 2017). She is genuflecting: the GIDS is perfectly aware that transgender is a historically specific phenomenon and that the meaning of trans is constantly shaped and re-shaped, including by the GIDS itself. The GIDS is unapologetic that it is "in the business of helping actively construct the idea and the understanding of transgender" and "actively helping to configure transgender in our time" (Wren, 2014, pp. 284, 286). As an institution dedicated to postmodern concepts, it admits transgender "*rests on no foundation of truth*" (Wren, 2014, p. 287, my emphasis).

The media, the internet, and organisations like Mermaids and Gendered Intelligence which are employed by many schools in the UK to provide workshops about 'gender identity' for schoolteachers and children as young as four, collectively provide the background to girls' everyday lives and deprive them of the language to speak of their distress other than through trans concepts. In combination, these influences construct a definitive set of 'truths' about 'gender identity' which reproduce a catalogue of gender stereotypes that confirm to girls that they *are* transgender, that medical re-assignment of their sexed body *will* resolve gender discomfort, and that without social and physical intervention they will be likely to self-harm and probably commit suicide. By the time they reach the GIDS, many girls, particularly those in whom onset of gender dysphoria has been rapid, already refract their confusions about gender through an unassailable trans identity (Littman, 2018).

The GIDS, in tandem with pro-trans lobby groups, instrumentalises a normalising classification of a person — the 'transboy' — which binds the girl even more tightly to the gender stereotypes which have helped contribute to her alleged identity as 'male' in the first place. Hormone therapy and future surgery are not benign technologies, as Wren implies, that help the young person 'assigned female at birth' to become 'his' authentic true self. On the alleged basis of a girl 'knowing her body', 'knowing what is right for her individually' and of her human rights to self-actualisation, the GIDS constructs the 'transboy' and facilitates the very fragmentation of her identity and dislocation from her body that is allegedly alleviated by a trans affirmative approach.

Now authorised by the GIDS, the 'transboy' goes on to be co-created in a circular fashion by legislation, transactivist rhetoric, politicians, and by some parents who have little option but to believe the NHS advice that transgenderism results from a mismatch between "the sex" to which their children were "assigned at birth" and the child's "inner sense of knowing" whether they are a boy or girl (Department of Health, 2008, p. 13). The idea is promulgated that girls can become men and that medical intervention is an opportunity for them to reject the constrictions of their female bodies to become their true authentic 'masculine' selves.

The body

The Memorandum of Understanding on Conversion, which many healthcare professionals have signed, purports to protect the patient from conversion therapy (see Chapter One). This Memorandum implies that "there is a fixed category called 'transgender' which, like eye colour, is simply a given that need not be thought about or understood" (Evans, 2020a, p. 2). However, children's sexual orientation and 'gender identity' are formed out of a complex developmental process that involves an interaction between their body, their mind and society. Sexual identity and gender identity are developmental processes that evolve as the individual goes through the different life stages (Evans, 2020a, p. 2).

The belief that transgender identity is located 'in the body' now permeates multiple aspects of our culture: media popularisation; educational curricula in schools; advice given by NHS to parents; and the GIDS itself. Collectively, these provide the background to children's everyday lives and combine to construct for them a definitive set of 'truths'. These 'truths' reproduce gender stereotypes that confirm to children they *must* be transgender, that medical re-assignment will resolve acute discomfort, and that without hormone 'therapy' they will be likely to self-harm and probably commit suicide.

Through postmodern disdain for the biological reality of dimorphic sex, and the queer language of 'assigned sex at birth', the girl seeks coherence through the unrealisable fantasy that she will be able to change sex. Cross-sex hormones will rob her of her future ability to become a mother, to have sexual pleasure without pain, to be free of a lifetime of dependency on the NHS and the unknown long-term risks of unlicensed drugs. And she will *never* become male or have the genitals of the other sex. Surgery on female bodies to produce a penis cannot create a functioning and sensate organ. The exogenous sex-related hormones will only create the *appearance* of sexual characteristics that differ from those her body would produce in the absence of intervention. Her human body is a whole organism which will constantly seek homeostasis (i.e. the tendency towards a relatively stable equilibrium between interdependent elements, especially as maintained by physiological processes). Interventions, whether surgical or hormonal, *cannot* actually create the desired sexed body, but can only modify the appearance and functioning of her own sexed body.

The idea that sex — whether the child is female or male — is socially constructed — and that trans is a *human* problem merely promotes the "illusion of inclusion" (Raymond, 1980, p. xxi). A woman is assimilated by this men's rights movement in much the same way that girls and women are assimilated into other male-defined realities — "on men's terms" (Raymond, 1980, p. xxi). Janice Raymond says that "transmen neutralise themselves" and are "not only neutralised but neutered" (Raymond, 1980, p. xxv). The neutering of women is not aberrant but on a continuum in the patriarchal attempt to control "female energy, spirit and vitality" (Raymond, 1980, xvi). History testifies to the brutal control of female flesh through foot binding, clitoridectomy and infibulation (the latter are still practiced within some cultures), hysterectomies, radical mastectomies, oophorectomies etc. to restore patriarchal social order (Raymond, 1980, p. xvi). When surgeons performed clitoridectomies and oophorectomies on women in the past, they solicited women's acceptance and collusion. Similarly, the young woman who now undergoes hormone treatment and medical surgery is 'voluntarily' divesting herself of the last traces of female identification. Raymond suggests that for a woman to castrate herself through surgery in order to become male is "the ultimate weapons in the hands of the boys" (1980, p. xxv).

Detransitioners: Kiera Bell

In February 2020, a challenge to the legality of hormone blocking and cross-sex hormone treatment for under 18-year-olds at the GIDS was mounted. Three people filed papers asking for a review: a former GIDS psychiatric nurse; the mother of a 15-year-old girl with autism who is on the GIDS' waiting list; Keira Bell, a 23-year-old woman and former 'transboy' helped by the GIDS to transition to a 'man' who has now detransitioned. A judicial review was granted on the basis of the claim that the hormone treatment is unlawful as the children in question cannot, by reference to Gillick criteria, validly give consent to a treatment which is both life-changing and likely to be irreversible. The review is now scheduled to take place in October 2020.

Kiera Bell, a young lesbian woman, is a textbook example of the girls presenting at the GIDS (Holt, 2020). She was referred at the age of sixteen, deeply distressed about her sexed body, and desperate to transition from female to male. After only three one-hour-long appointments she claims that she was prescribed puberty blockers; one year later she was prescribed testosterone; three years ago, at the age of twenty she underwent a double mastectomy; last year she decided to stop taking testosterone and says she now accepts her sex as female.

Bell's teenage identification as male gradually built up as she found out more about transitioning online (Holt, 2020). As she proceeded down the medical route, "one step led to another" and although she now says she wouldn't have wanted to listen to voices of caution, no one actually challenged her. She was allowed to run with the fantasy that she could change sex and that hormone treatment would save her from suicidal ideation and depression. Alongside her purported gender dysphoria, she strongly believed sex transition would relieve all her mental health issues stemming from a difficult home life and feeling unaccepted by society (Holt, 2020). She is angry about what has happened to her during the last decade and incensed that the GIDS facilitated medical transition so readily.

Dr Polly Carmichael made a confident and bold but disingenuous statement to the media in response to the Bell case. She said that detransitioners amount to less than 3% of young people who have transitioned (Carmichael, 2020). In fact, the actual numbers of those who detransition are as yet unknown and difficult to assess for many reasons, including that transitioned girls are just coming into adulthood now (Butler and Hutchinson, 2020, p. 45). Moreover, for those of us who have been researching transgender body politics for some years, we know that many young women privately detransition but are afraid to make it publicly known because they experience the transgender community as a cult from which they are afraid to extricate themselves and become socially excommunicated (Robbins, 2019). Carmichael could have proffered some concrete evidence, namely that around four-fifths of young children grow out of trans identification naturally if not assisted by gender development identity services (Butler and Hutchinson, 2020, p. 46).

Marcus Evans argues that the "political, rights-based approach to the treatment of children" such as that practised by the GIDS "is at risk of forcing [children and young people's] complex psychological needs into the background" (Evans, 2020a, p. 3). The radical disconnection of children's discomfort about gender from its potential roots in psychological and sociological phenomena has been fiercely promoted by pro-trans lobbies, who label clinicians as 'transphobic' if they insist on a thorough assessment of young people's familial and psychological background. Clinicians who are trying to protect the child from embarking prematurely on irreversible treatment are "rebranded as a malign influence getting in the way of what the child 'needs'" (Evans, 2020a, p. 4). Evans points out it is "clear that this politically driven culture interferes with the freedom of thought necessary to work with these very troubled children and adolescents ... they become political symbols, actors in a wider ideological conflict" (Evans, 2020a, p. 4). He concludes that the GIDS has been "functioning as if acting outside the ordinary requirement of good medical and psychiatric practice ... [and] requires a new regulator tasked with appropriate oversight of gender identity services to ensure a more clinically rigorous, balanced and ethical approach to this complex area" (Evans, 2020a, p. 4).

In conclusion, Big Pharma is a capitalist enterprise deeply invested in the medical technologies that help *create and shape* the girl's self-identification as male. The GIDS (and other international Gender Identity Development Services in the world) provide the global marketplace for Big Pharma's profiteering. The Care Quality Commission,[7] which rated the GIDS system as 'good', has been working with Stonewall since 2012 as part of their Health Champions Scheme. The Tavistock and Portman NHS Trust is also a Stonewall Health Champion (Transgender Trend, 2020). While health and educational institutions remain captured by the ideology of Stonewall, Mermaids and Gendered Intelligence, and while all practices of transgendering children can be traced back to an extremely powerful multi-million dollar medical-industrial complex, it behooves the UK government and the governments of all other democratic countries to thoroughly examine the theories, politics and money that underpin them.

Citizens should be able to ask without reprisal: Who has the right to make knowledge about sex and gender which then informs paediatric clinical practice? How free are clinical psychologists and other medical professionals to 'first do no

---

7   The Care Quality Commission is an executive non-departmental public body of the Department of Health and Social Care, UK, established in 2009 to regulate and inspect health and social care services in England (Care Quality Commission, 2020).

harm', given the force field of transgender meaning-making and trans lobbyists' assumed authority about human rights? What is the relationship between the exponential rise in girls identifying as boys and misogyny, sexism and sexual violence?

I argue that a militant trans activism positively requires 'trans children' to exist as natural figures in order to fabricate the illusion that transgender identity is apolitical. The human being most sacrificed on the altar of queer theory and a burgeoning men's rights movement is the new medicalised identity: 'The Transboy'. The idea is promulgated that girls can become men and that medical intervention is an opportunity for them to reject the constrictions of their female bodies to become their true authentic 'masculine' selves. Since 'gender identity' has been successfully untethered by pro-trans lobby groups from its social and political context and is increasingly conceptualised as an inherent quality, girls will continue to be caught up in socially constructed gender-based oppression. The sterilisation of girls in the name of gender freedom does not signify the extension of their human rights, but constitutes their egregious breach.

Chapter Three
The Male Body Politic

3.1 Queering the Law and Social Policy

In 2015, Conservative Member of Parliament (MP) Maria Miller headed a newly constituted governmental Select Committee for Women and Equalities. The very first piece of work that the Committee carried out was an inquiry into trans inequality (Women and Equalities Committee Report, 2016). The Committee had sought to interview a number of stakeholders, including Stonewall, Gendered Intelligence and Mermaids, and one of the most influential trans lobbyists in the UK: Stephen Whittle, Professor of Equalities Law, a previous President of the World Professional Association of Transgender Health (WPATH),[8] queer theorist and an active member of the UK trans lobby group Press for Change. Moreover, Whittle was deployed in a further capacity as the Committee's *specialist* advisor, the suitability for which includes Whittle's previous collaboration

---

8   Whittle was President Elect of WPATH 2005-2007, President 2007-2009, and Officer 2009-2011 (WPATH, 2020). See Chapter Two for criticisms of WPATH's Standards of Care (which inform NHS England guidelines for the GIDS) as clinically unsafe and unsuitable for public health care gender clinics.

with the government on transsexual/transgender rights (Home
Office, 2000).

Whittle has had a disproportionate effect on the British body
politic. Born female and transitioning as a young adult woman
in her twenties, Whittle almost single-handedly initiated the
process of the legal replacement of sex with 'gender identity' as a
fundamental issue of human rights not only for trans identifying
people but for gender non-conforming children (Brunskell-
Evans, 2019). In 2007, Whittle was part of a self-appointed group
of scholars/transactivists/human rights 'experts' who produced
a civil society document delineating a set of legal principles,
known as the Yogyakarta Principles,[9] for the application of
international law to human rights violations based on 'gender
identity'. In this document, 'gender identity' is defined as

> ... each person's deeply felt internal and individual experience of
> gender, which may or may not correspond with the sex assigned at
> birth, including the personal sense of the body (which may involve,
> if freely chosen, modification of bodily appearance or function by
> medical, surgical or other means) and other expressions of gender,

---

9   Though not legally binding, the Yogyakarta Principles have been
     understood as an authoritative interpretation of international law and
     provide a definitional point for academic papers, bills, resolutions and
     other documents (see Scottish Government, 2017; Human Rights Watch,
     2007; and Agius and Tobler, 2011). They are not incorporated into any
     UN convention or declaration, yet they are regularly cited and used as a
     reference point in the UN (Ettlebrick and Zeran, 2011). Equality and human
     rights legislation has been updated and created in states across the western
     world that incorporates 'gender identity' as a component part of legal
     personhood and presumes that the right to self-defined 'gender identity'
     encompasses all aspects of anti-discrimination law with regard to sex and
     gender.

including dress, speech and mannerisms (Yogyakarta Principles, 2007).

Transgender rights are defined as politically progressive and intersectional with the rights of other oppressed or marginalised groups, including the human rights of women:

> ... all human rights are universal, interdependent, indivisible and interrelated ... and gender identity [is] integral to every person's dignity and humanity and must not be the basis for discrimination or abuse (Yogyakarta Principles, 2007).

The bias of the Transgender Equality Report is that its specialist advisor came to the table as a polemicist. Since 'gender identity' is unverifiable and has no physical manifestation such as chromosomal sex or genitalia, but refers to a person's deeply 'felt' internal experience, demonstrated through stereotypes of femininity and masculinity, 'gender identity' is de-politicised and naturalised. There is an absence of explanation for how gender is related to sex such that there is an alleged correspondence for 'cisgender' people with their 'sex assigned at birth' in contrast to a non-correspondence for transgender people. The open-ended linkage between biological sex and modification of the body suggests that sex is a mutable social construct that can change by modifying bodily structure and function, and is irrelevant to other forms of discrimination, for example sex discrimination.

Oral evidence was also provided to the Committee by a panel of trans people speaking about their wish for law reform, and by Drs Carmichael and Wren from the GIDS who, as we saw in the previous chapter, are single minded in their view that science has to take a back seat to the 'human right' of unhappy children to 'know' the solution to their gender misery. No women's groups were consulted as special witnesses (Women and Equalities Committee Report, 2016). These partisan, ideological views were embedded in the Report and its recommendations for how to achieve equality for trans adults and children and have been responsible for the subsequent abuse of women and children's rights.

It was almost inevitable that the conclusion to this allegedly thorough, objective inquiry was commensurate with what the narrow range of witnesses deemed necessary, namely the reform of the *Gender Recognition Act 2004* (GRA) (Government Legislation UK, 2020c). The Committee was told that although originally deemed groundbreaking, the GRA had not gone far enough with regard to trans rights. The GRA, it concluded, puts unnecessary and punitive procedural difficulties and legal hurdles in front of a trans person which impede them from being recognised as their 'true' gender identity.

The *Gender Recognition Act 2004*

Before 2004, in order to be legally recognised as female in the UK, a man (and at this time it was overwhelmingly men seeking to transition) had to have undergone genital surgery. The GRA accomplished a substantive milestone on the trajectory of self-identification away from the body as the determinant of whether one is a man or a woman by stating: "If the acquired *gender* is the male gender, the person's *sex* becomes that of a man and, if it is the female *gender*, the person's *sex* becomes that of a woman"

(*Gender Recognition Act* section 9.1). One of the people central to that shift is Stephen Whittle. Since the late twentieth century there had been a sustained international trans campaign to replace the category sex with 'gender identity' in law in which Whittle had played an instrumental role. His international collaborations as well as domestic lobbying laid the grounds for the conceptual work that the GRA accomplished for how sex is legally defined (Brunskell-Evans, 2019).

The GRA enables trans people (over the age of eighteen), without the requirement of genital surgery, to procure a Gender Recognition Certificate (GRC) in order to obtain a new birth certificate recording an M or F just the same as if that had been their sex at birth. Certain stipulations are linked to gaining a GRC, including an individual demonstrating to a panel that they have a medical diagnosis of gender dysphoria, have been living for a period of two years in the gender they wished their new birth certificate to reflect, and intend to live in their 'acquired' gender for the rest of their life.

Whittle celebrates the fact that the GRA effectively demolishes the sex/gender distinction "both literally and legally." This is the historical moment when, for the first time, 'gender identity' "becomes and *defines* legal sex" (Whittle and Turner, 2007, section 1.5). Since the passing of the Act "legal sex transformations can now be literally disembodied" (Whittle and Turner, 2007, section 1.5). Whittle describes the GRA "as performative in Butler's sense of the term: ... as a form of speech-act it makes gender into sex in law" (Whittle and Turner, 2007, section 1.5). The Act offers trans people who *do* identify as men or women, the right to be legally recognised as such "even if one is a woman with a penis or a man with a vagina" (Whittle and Turner, 2007, section 1.5).

Witnesses to the Committee contended that trans people's human rights to live authentic lives are impeded by a legal system that does not afford them parity with 'cis' people. The internal sense of 'gender identity' as the marker of whether one is male or female is not a pathology and needs erasing from the GRA in favour of *self-declared 'gender identity'* in order to 'scale up' transgender people to parity and equality with their 'cis' peers (see Chapter One).

The Committee ascertained that, as an issue of social justice, trans people want all gatekeeping to self-identification waived. While the GRA had been a pioneering piece of legislation in 2004, in its view it still pathologises trans people and runs contrary to their dignity and personal autonomy. As a consequence, without any awareness of the deeply ideological nature of the political battle previously waged and founded on Judith Butler's queer theory, the Committee's request for self-identification was granted as reasonable. The report recommended the following reforms of the GRA:

1. A simple administrative process of self-declaration of 'gender identity' without the need for a medical diagnosis, including reducing the age to 16/17-year-olds;
2. A person with a GRC should never be excluded from a single-sex occupation or service for people of their acquired gender; and

3. The protected characteristic of the *Equality Act 2010* should be changed from 'gender reassignment' to 'gender identity'. (I shall return to this point later.)

In 2018, the then Minister for Women and Equalities and Secretary of State for International Development, Penny Mordaunt, led the attempt to reform the GRA by launching a public consultation. In doing so, she was responding to an outcry from women in 2017 who were becoming alert to the possible impact on women's rights of the newly constructed right of men to self-identify as women. The Preface to the public consultation documentation first establishes the Conservative Government's credentials as supporters of LGBT rights. We are told that in order to mitigate the barriers to full equality, the government had already committed three million pounds to help tackle transphobic bullying in schools, funded the NHS Gender Identity Development Service, and conducted one of the largest national surveys of LGBT people in the world (GOV.UK, 2018). It goes on to make clear the outcome the Government would like the consultation to achieve, namely "how the Government might make it easier for trans people to achieve legal recognition" (GOV.UK, 2018). The document describes 'gender identity' as "A person's internal sense of their own gender. This does not have to be a man or woman. It could be, for example, non-binary" (GOV.UK, 2018). Mordaunt says, "the consultation marks a significant step in this Government's work to advance equality for LGBT people" (GOV.UK, 2018). This statement is factually incorrect in that the government had *not* been proactive in advancing the equality of lesbians, gay men or bisexual people. But now the transactivist movement has successfully linked T with LGB which is a conceptual coup that gives the appearance of homogenous and collective interests of these four groups. In fact their interests are very different: being lesbian, gay or bisexual is a *sexual orientation*; being transgender is referring to a non-definable *'gender identity'*.

In recommending far-reaching legal changes in a liberal democracy that redefine 'woman' without acknowledging the profound public policy implications of that change on women (and girls), the government demonstrated:

1. a serious lack of consciousness of the ideas they were embracing and helping reproduce;
2. inadequate institutional safeguards against well-organised and highly purposeful single-issue lobbying groups such as Stonewall, Gendered Intelligence and Mermaids in firstly determining social policy and secondly representing a constituency — trans identifying people — which makes up less than 1% of the population (Gendered Intelligence, 2020b); and
3. a predisposed partisanship to the transgender human rights paradigm that is so strong that women, who make up more than 50% of the population, had no representation in redefining the category to which they belong.

'Feminist' politicians speak with one voice

In October 2017, then Prime Minister Theresa May became the first serving prime minister to attend the PinkNews Awards. PinkNews is a UK-based online newspaper for "the global LGBT+ community" whose "mission is to inform, inspire change and empower people to be themselves" (PinkNews, 2020). The awards were the chosen location for her announcement that the Government would seek to "streamline and de-medicalise" the process of changing gender to reflect that "being trans is not an illness" (Cary, 2017). In too many cases, May pointed out, the current system prevents trans people from acquiring legal recognition "of who they are, denying them the dignity and respect that comes with it" (GOV.UK, 2018).

In November 2018, Mordaunt gave a speech at the Women MPs of the World event in the House of Commons where she said that "transgender women" belong to the category of "the most marginalised of women" (Mordaunt, 2018). In the same year, Sophie Walker, then leader of the Women's Equality Party, divested one of its nationally elected spokeswomen — me! — of my role within the Party when an allegation of transphobia was brought against me by a self-identified transwoman within our membership. In November 2017, I had expressed a view on BBC Radio 4 that sex is a material reality, gender is socially constructed, and that boys and girls should be allowed to express themselves without restriction, but not allowed to medically transition till they are legally adult (Brunskell-Evans, 2017). Although this was such a mild thing to say, the complainant immediately, without censure from the Party, accused me on social media of Nazism, and even, since it was the eve of The Transgender Day of Remembrance, of contributing to an atmosphere which leads to the murder of trans people (Brunskell-Evans, 2018a). I was placed under investigation, including being subjected to an interview that lasted approximately three hours. I was asked to sign a confidentiality agreement but refused. Thankfully, I had taken two witnesses with me — a veteran feminist and a young medical doctor.

By late February 2018, I attended a Woman's Place UK (WPUK) meeting. The complainant commented the following day that the meeting "was stuck in a time warp like the SS. No-one is erasing women, transwomen are women and have been since the beginning of time" (Brunskell-Evans, 2018a). Presumably referring to me, he continued: "The WEP needs to ensure this cancer is removed" (Brunskell-Evans, 2018a). The complainant's accusations of transphobia were upheld by the WEP (Women's Equality Party). *The Times* journalist Janice Turner (Turner, 2018) describes how "even a party for women won't take on the trans lobby." She says reform of the GRA had already become

> ... an incendiary feminist issue, yet the WEP cannot even debate it. Brunskell-Evans's views were anodyne enough to be broadcast on the BBC at teatime, but the WEP sacked her because a single transgender member complained (Turner, 2018).

In 2018, Dawn Butler, Shadow Minister for Women and Equalities in the Labour Party, insisted that "trans women are women" and saw no reason why they should not enter the party's all-women shortlists for parliamentary seats (Boycott-Owen,

2018). In 2019, Nicola Sturgeon, First Minister of Scotland, said that as an "ardent, passionate feminist," she doesn't see "the greater recognition of transgender rights" as a threat to her "as a woman" or to her "feminism" (Paton, 2019). While speaking on human rights at the United Nations, Sturgeon announced that

> Scotland has plans to bring forward legislation to simplify the process around gender recognition. It doesn't change the fundamentals. It simply makes that process easier. And, I hope, intends to put more dignity into that process for people who are going through the process of changing their gender (Paton, 2019).

In identifying themselves as feminist, these politicians have aligned themselves with intersectional feminism (discussed in Chapter 1) that is rooted in the following fundamental principles: transwomen *are* women; the category women is sub-divided and the struggles of 'cis women' and 'trans women' do not compete but intersect; supporting reform of the GRA is synonymous with support for 'trans rights' and progressivism; and finally, opposing reforms is synonymous with transphobia.

The erosion of single-sex spaces

Stonewall's submission to the Women & Equalities Select Committee Inquiry on Transgender Equality had called for "A review of the *Equality Act 2010* to include 'gender identity' rather than 'gender reassignment' as a protected characteristic and to remove exemptions, such as access to single-sex spaces" (Stonewall, 2015).

Similarly, Gendered Intelligence's submission states in its executive summary, "We need a comprehensive review of the legislation affecting trans people (and intersex people) with the aim of deleting the exceptions laid out in the GRA 2004 and EA 2010" (Gendered Intelligence, 2015).

In 2015, before any consultation had begun, and hot on the heels of the Committee's recommendations, the Government Equalities Office (GEO) produced a guide in partnership with Jay Stewart, which sets out guidance and good practice for anyone providing statutory, voluntary sector or business/commercial services to the public e.g. shops, restaurants, public houses, banks, sports clubs and leisure centres. Its avowed purpose was to help service providers comply with the law as set out in the *Equality Act 2010* with regard to gender reassignment as a protected characteristic. Trans people include

> ... those who may describe themselves as transsexual, transgender, a cross-dresser (transvestite), non-binary and anyone else who may not conform to traditional gender roles. It includes those who have transitioned from male to female (transgender women) or from female to male (transgender men) as well as those who do not have a typically 'male' or 'female' gender identity (non-binary) (Government Equality Office, 2015, p. 4).

The GEO describes 'gender reassignment' as occurring when a person takes steps to alter the outward expression of their gender so that it better aligns with their sense of who they are or, in other words, their identity as they see it (Government Equality Office, 2015, p. 4). According to the GEO, as part of their gender reassignment, some people may choose to take hormones and/

or have surgery, but medical intervention is not an essential part of gender reassignment. A trans person should be free to select the facilities (such as toilets or changing rooms) appropriate to the gender in which they present. For example, when a trans person starts to live in their acquired gender on a full-time basis, they should be afforded the right to use the facilities appropriate to their acquired gender. And service providers must avoid discriminating against anyone with the protected characteristic of 'gender reassignment' (Government Equality Office, 2015, p. 4).

The promotion by the government of gender self-identification in an unregulated form, such as that achieved by the GEO and Jay Stewart, ahead of any changes to the law, had a substantial impact across public service providers. The 'gender' a man identifies as having — not the sex one has by birth, or even by law — became the determinant of whether he may permissibly enter women-only spaces. From prisons to youth hostels to colleges to changing rooms to swimming pools to shared train sleeper carriages to hospital wards, self-identification has become the *de facto* criterion of entry. In 2017, the trans performer Travis Alabanza made a formal complaint to a well-known High Street store that he had been denied entry to the women's changing rooms and thus been discriminated against. The store changed its national policy defining that they are "open to all persons, regardless of gender identity of expression" (Petter, 2017).

All political parties and political leaders supported the roll-out of these societal changes which were transforming what it is to be a woman and who could be included in that category. In 2018, the National Executive Committee, the ruling body of the Labour Party (the then and current opposition party in the UK) ruled that men who self-identify as women are eligible for all-women shortlists, minimum quotas for women, and other positions such as Constituency Party Women's Officer, a role designed to facilitate equality of opportunity for females in a male-dominated organisation (Waugh, 2018). Dawn Butler, the Party's then shadow Secretary of State for Women and Equalities, insisted that 'transwomen' can fill designated roles for women, arguing that any other view was equivalent to homophobia (Necati, 2018). As early as 2017, the consequences of the Labour Party's approach had already emerged. Lily Madigan, a 19-year-old teenager formerly known as Liam, was elected as the Women's Officer for a Labour Party branch (Rochester and Strood in Kent), a post specifically designated for women. Shockingly, he had earlier called for the sacking of Anne Ruzylo, a female Labour Party Women's Officer in a different constituency, for being 'transphobic'. Although the complaint was eventually dismissed, the effect of this male teenager's interference was to rid the Labour Party of a female constituency Women's Officer as Anne Ruzylo resigned.[10]

---

10 Anne Ruzylo, Labour Party local Women's Officer for Bexhill and Battle, a lesbian and trade unionist, had criticised "the sanctification of the trans movement" (Whelan, 2017). For this, she was labelled a TERF by Madigan and was harassed by transgender activists online (Whelan, 2017; Bannerman, 2017). It formed part of a wider transphobia campaign which in part prompted the resignation of Ruzylo and the rest of the executive committee in support of her (Whelan, 2017; Bannerman, 2017).

By 2019, Mordaunt's office was already issuing guidelines telling businesses and public sector agencies that they should allow people to access 'single sex' facilities such as communal changing rooms and dormitories based on their self-identified gender, not their physical sex. In its own internal equal opportunities monitoring it had already stopped asking about sex altogether (Forstater, 2019). At a conference at the Stonewall Workplace Conference London in April 2019, Mordaunt thanked everyone who had worked and continues to work in and with Stonewall for their "hard work" and "commitment ... fighting for justice"

> ... with our four nations radically in different places on social policy, and LGBT issues in particular ... you're vital to forming the social fabric of our United Kingdom ... it's about our national identity, it's about our national values, and our potential, as individuals and as a country (Mordaunt, 2019).

A Woman's Place is standing her ground

Since 2015, women in the UK had been witnessing the rapid erosion of their sex-based legal protections because access to single-sex facilities had become governed by a principle of self-identification in almost all cases, as described above. If anyone can identify as a woman, and be treated as if they *are* women, they effectively have access to women's safe spaces on demand (changing rooms, refuges, hospital wards, prisons and so on), then there is potential risk of men abusing such open access. Either women exist as one half of a sexually dimorphic species that are vulnerable to the other half because of their reproductive biology and their social standing, or women do not exist as a biological category and therefore there is no need for protections.

Woman's Place UK (WPUK) became vocal in 2017 to discuss the implications and possible impact on women's rights. WPUK describes itself as a women's rights organisation which consists of people from a range of backgrounds including trade unions, women's organisations, academia and the NHS (WPUK, 2020). It was the first organisation to provide a space where women (including 'transwomen') could discuss the possible ramifications of allowing men to change their legal sex based only on making a legally registered self-declaration. Many other laudable women's organisations sprang up at the same time, but none with quite the public reach that WPUK has achieved.

WPUK was concerned that reform of the GRA would fundamentally undermine the principles underpinning sex as a protected characteristic of the *Equality Act 2010* (Government Legislation, 2020). The Act places specific duties on service providers and public bodies to consider the needs of particular groups of people who share protected characteristics. The two protected characteristics which concern us here are 'sex' and — for the first time in law — 'gender reassignment.'

With regard to sex, section 7 of the *Equality Act 2010* states the protected characteristic of sex refers to a person who is "a man" or "a woman" and a reference to persons who share a protected characteristic is a reference to "persons of the same sex" (Government Legislation UK, 2020a). The principles underlying the need for the protection of women are that the physical and social consequences of being female are so significant that women need specific protections in law and policy. Sex-based disadvantages may relate directly to female biology, for example, pregnancy and maternity discrimination, while sexual violence and domestic abuse can be related to the lower status ascribed to the female sex class. The special measures create equality of opportunity in a sexist world with protections designed to redress abuse, inequality and discrimination suffered by women (Murray and Hunter Blackburn, 2019). With regard to 'gender reassignment', the principles underlying the need for the protection lie in social stigma and discrimination. A person has a protected characteristic in section 7 of the *Equality Act 2010* if s/he is "proposing to undergo, is undergoing or has undergone a process (or part of a process) for the purpose of reassigning the person's sex by changing physiological or other attributes" (Government Legislation, 2020b).

Audrey Ludwig, a practising discrimination solicitor, points out that the way the 'trans rights debate' is portrayed by lobbyists, most politicians, many corporates and the media, is legally wrong (Ludwig, 2020). The 'trans rights debate', in terms of equality law, isn't about rights for trans people not to be discriminated against or harassed unlawfully because they are trans. Properly, that right is already contained under the protected characteristic of 'gender reassignment', and covers people anywhere along the 'transition' route whether they have had hormones, surgery, or not, and whether they even progress down that route or not. The feminist argument is a sex-based rights one about who comes within the class of men or women in section 11 of the Equality Act and it is this issue with which WPUK was concerned, *not* eroding the rights of protection for people who wish to transition (Ludwig, 2020).

WPUK was worried that if 'gender re-assignment' is replaced by 'gender identity' and encoded in law, as the Select Committee for Women and Equalities had proposed, then a man without any medical diagnosis of dysphoria or other substantive constraints, could have access to sex-segregated spaces and women's sex-based rights will be rendered impossible to enforce. In policy-making, when the concept of gender, as a subjective matter of self-identity, takes precedence over sex, the special measures introduced by the *Equality Act 2010* are undermined.

WPUK set out core aims. These are:

1. Respectful and evidence-based discussion about the impact of the proposed reforms and for women's voices to be heard;
2. The principle of women-only spaces to be upheld — and where necessary extended;
3. A review of how the exemptions in the *Equality Act* which allow for single-sex services or requirements that only a woman can apply for a job (such as in a domestic violence refuge) are being applied in practice;
4. Government to consult with women's organisations on how self-declaration would impact on women-only services and spaces;
5. Government to consult on how self-declaration will impact upon data gathering — such as crime, employment, pay

and health statistics — and monitoring of sex-based discrimination such as the gender pay gap (WPUK, 2020).

These moderate aims, all of which are part of orthodox legal frameworks and into ordinary protocols for proposed changing of legislation, are defined by transactivists and trans lobbyists as so extreme that WPUK is now publicly defamed as a 'hate organisation.' In the past three years when WPUK have organised meetings, the organisers, speakers and attendees have been routinely vilified (and worse) as bigots and transphobes (WPUK, 2020). Every single meeting that WPUK has organised has faced a campaign of harassment and was targeted by violence and abuse, including accusations of transphobia (WPUK, 2018).

For the sake of brevity three examples are illustrative. The first WPUK meeting in 2017 encountered a form of opposition that would prove not only typical for further events, but sadly revealed political dynamics which would escalate over the ensuing years. The meeting was held in response to a threat to women's right to speak. The four women concerned were: Linda Bellos, a leading UK feminist, Labour Party activist and pioneer of anti-racist policies who had had an invitation withdrawn to speak at Cambridge University amid concerns that transgender activists opposed her being platformed (Bannerman, 2017a); Helen Steel, a Green Party member and environmental and social justice campaigner who was physically threatened and surrounded at London Anarchist Book Fair for defending women distributing leaflets about the proposed reform of the GRA (Steel, 2017, 2018); Anne Ruzylo, discussed above, who had been subjected to harassment in her role as Women's Officer of the Labour Party; and myself, who had been divested by the WEP of my spokeswoman role for expressing my views on BBC's Radio 4. At this meeting, WPUK experienced its first orchestrated campaign to prevent the meeting from going ahead. A message was received saying, "If ISIS only blow up one event this Christmas ..." and although WPUK assumed this person wasn't connected with ISIS, "it did confirm that some feel violence against women wishing to speak on gender is justified" (WPUK, 2017).

In 2018, WPUK faced a well-organised attempt by Oxford University student activists to shut down a meeting held in the Oxford Meeting House of The Society of Friends (Quakers) (WPUK, 2018). The speakers included Stephanie Davies-Arai, founder of Transgender Trend, Nic Williams, founder of Fair Play for Women, and Raquel Rosario Sánchez, a Bristol University PhD student from the Dominican Republic researching sexual violence towards women. After this WPUK meeting, The Society of Friends (Quakers),[11] otherwise noted

---

11 Quaker Bookshop UK (https://bookshop.quaker.org.uk/) has a section dedicated to queer theory, including books by authors/lobbyists who affirm the medical transitioning of children, for example Burns (2018), or which feature the queer theorist Gayle Rubin, for example Barker and Scheele (2016). Rubin describes breaking the social taboo against "intergenerational sex" (child sexual abuse) as a form of sexual liberation for the child and the adult (Rubin, 1982, p. 282). At the same time, the bookshop refuses to stock Brunskell-Evans and Moore (2018), a book concerned with safeguarding children from medical intervention. The grounds for refusal are that it will make people who identify as trans and who work for Quakers "feel unsafe" (personal correspondence).

for peaceful dialogue, and currently running a programme that facilitates negotiation between Palestinians and Israelis, accepted the narrative that WPUK is a 'hate group' and ceased offering meeting houses as venues, and, astonishingly, even refused dialogue with one of the WPUK founders.[12]

Lastly, in September 2019, WPUK held its 24th public meeting in two years, timed to coincide with the Labour Party's annual conference and to publicise its manifesto (WPUK, 2019a) which contains demands to significantly improve the quality of women's lives, as well as address structural oppression and discrimination (WPUK, 2019a, 2019b). A protest of approximately 100 people outside the building had ticket holders brave a narrow corridor surrounded by aggressive protestors taking photos, shouting "SCUM! SCUM! SCUM!" "TERF! TERF! TERF" and "SHAME ON YOU" while the police watched. Attendees were made up of ordinary women, including survivors of sexual and domestic violence, as well as Labour Party members who had specifically attended the meeting as one of the conference fringe events. Sheets had to be pinned up at the door and windows to stop protestors taking photos of women within the building. The demonstrators banged on the windows of the hall throughout, in an attempt to make the meeting impossible. The audience refused to be intimidated and the expected two-hour meeting continued. Several Labour Party delegates subsequently made false accusations at their own conference about WPUK from the podium, which went unchecked by the Chair (WPUK, 2019b).

---

12 Quakers also employ Mermaids as trainers for adults/young people who work with children and teenagers at Quaker gatherings and social events.

In conclusion, public meetings, where women have a right to speak, be heard and challenged have had to be held in secret or, when the location is discovered, attendees are subject to harassment and threats of violence (Peak Trans, 2020; WPUK, 2020). Shockingly, the misogyny directed at women and the violence perpetrated by transactivists against women remain uncommented on and tacitly tolerated by mainstream media, religious bodies and human rights organisations. While women are repeatedly commanded/instructed to affirm the right of 'transwomen' to be included in the category 'women', there is never a requirement of human rights organisations to acknowledge the level of violence and harassment that women face and state their opposition to sexist abuse. Or challenge the outrageous statements made by some trans advocates which repeatedly deny women's experiences and silence women's voices, a power imbalance based on the long held expectation in society that women should be subservient (Steel, 2017).

3.2 The Trans Human Rights Paradigm

Women's prisons

The inclusion of criminal men into women's prisons is a lens through which to examine the safety of women when a social policy prioritises gender self-identity over sex as the most significant determinant for prison authorities to decide in which prison — female or male — a prisoner will be held.

There are numerous issues that make the prison an important location: Prisons have always been segregated by sex because it has been understood that women (as a class) need protecting from predation by men (as a class) and that women prisoners have a different set of needs as well as a different patterns of criminal offending. Crime is highly gendered, particularly sexual and violent offending (Crown Prosecution Service, 2016). In England and Wales, there are 21 male prisoners for every female (Ministry of Justice, 2017). A far higher proportion of prisoners in the men's estate are convicted of sex offences: 98.5% of sexual offenders in prison are male. Conversely, there is evidence that women are more vulnerable to sexual predation: about 36% of women recall being sexually abused as children, compared to 6% of male prisoners; 57% of female inmates have been victims of domestic violence (Ministry of Justice, 2017).

The Women and Equalities Committee inquiry into transgender equality chaired by Maria Miller was provided with submitted written evidence from The British Association of Gender Identity Specialists (BAGIS), a group of clinicians and other health professionals committed to transgender healthcare, about the worrying motivations of some males who self-identify as women:

> It has been rather naïvely suggested that nobody would seek to pretend transsexual status in prison if this were not actually the case. There are, to those of us who actually interview the prisoners, in fact very many reasons why people might pretend this [including] a plethora of prison intelligence information suggesting that the driving force was a desire to make subsequent sexual offending very much easier (BAGIS, 2015).

This clear evidence suggests that some male sex-offending criminals have attempted to exploit already existing gender-change rules for harmful and illegitimate purposes, and that others are likely to attempt to do so in future. Unfortunately, the Committee ignored this written submission, concluding in favour of placing 'transwomen' in the female estate: "There is a clear risk of harm (including violence, sexual assault, self-harming and suicide) where trans prisoners are not located in a prison or other setting appropriate to their acquired/affirmed gender" (Women and Equalities Committee, 2016, p. 86).

In 2016, the Government, "committed to taking action to remove barriers to equality, including transgender equality," commissioned the Ministry of Justice to carry out a review into the care and management of transgender offenders (Ministry of Justice, 2016, p. 3). Revised prison regulations were based on the "independent oversight" of two external consultants, the Deputy Director of the Prison Reform Trust and Jay Stewart, Director of Gendered Intelligence (Ministry of Justice, 2016, p. 3). The review gathered evidence from "a wide range of stakeholders, including many in the transgender community, and met transgender prisoners serving both long and short sentences" (Ministry of Justice, 2016, p. 3). It concluded that, "[A]llowing transgender offenders to experience the system in the gender in which they identify will, in the great majority of cases, represent the most humane and safest way to act" (Ministry of Justice, 2016, p. 4).

No female prisoners who may be forced to live alongside male-born prisoners were consulted and no organisations specialising in advocacy work for women were involved in the review (Fair Play For Women, 2018). A new operational instruction was fully implemented in 2017 across all men's and women's prisons which meant, that for the first time, legally male prisoners with fully intact male bodies complete with a penis could be allowed to live freely alongside female inmates in one of the twelve women's prisons in England (Fair Play For Women, 2018).

The case of Karen White

Since 2017, UK prison policy has allowed male-born transgender inmates to be detained in women's prisons or to request transfer to a women's prison. These regulations allowed about two dozen males into the women's estate, one of whom was the rapist Karen White who went on to sexually assault two female prisoners. White had been denied bail and remanded to await trial to protect the public from his violence (Trans Crime UK, 2018). In 2018, he was convicted of committing three rapes, plus burglary and wounding, and two counts of sexual assault while held on remand. I do not know whether he was convicted as a man or a woman, but I do know that when sentencing him, Judge Christopher Batty deferred to White's chosen identity using female personal pronouns. During the hearing, the lawyers referred to White as a woman, using language such as 'her penis' to describe his assault on the women inmates (Trans Crime UK, 2018).

Following the outcry about the Karen White case, including by an organisation called Fair Play For Women (2018) which has consistently drawn attention to this as a women's rights issue, the Ministry of Justice has carried out a further review (Ministry of Justice, 2020). The re-issuing of a revised policy framework emphasises

> ... adopting a balanced approach which considers the safety and needs of those who are transgender, whilst ensuring that decisions do not negatively impact on the well-being and safety of others, particularly in custodial settings such as in women's prisons. ... any new polices developed because of this Policy Framework are compliant with the relevant legislation including the Public Sector Equality Duty (*Equality Act 2010*) (Ministry of Justice, 2020, pp. 1–2).

In private communication between the feminist blogger The Martian Anthropologist and Her Majesty's Prisons and Probation Service (HMPPS), HMPPS makes clear the review is not concerned with the fundamental premises of the policy itself: "The key principle underlying the instruction is that individuals should be cared for and managed in the gender with which they identify." The Prison Service "will always apply this principle" even though "there is no legal obligation to locate a transgender prisoner in a prison according to their self-declared gender" (The Martian Anthropologist, 2019). Despite the fact that there is no legal obligation, the HMPPS assures us that every individual case involves a detailed and time-consuming process:

> Decisions on transferring someone to a prison which does not match their birth gender [sic] can only be made on the recommendation of a 'Complex Case Board'. These boards will look at the overall management of the individual, including the most appropriate location, and any other measures which are necessary to manage any risks both to them and presented by them. External experts, such as healthcare providers or Gender Identity Clinics will be

involved, and all decisions are the responsibility of a senior prison manager (Martian Anthropologist, 2019).

Aside from the fact that the usual confusion has been made by HMPPS between sex and gender, so that gender replaces sex in 'birth gender', The Martian Anthropologist asks correctly: "If the prison service genuinely believes that men should be managed as women if they say they are women, why should the transfer to a women's prison be signed off by a Complex Case Board?" (Martian Anthropologist, 2019).

One in 50 male prisoners are now self-identifying as transgender, according to a survey by the official jail watchdog (Hymas, 2019). Transferring males to women's prisons has real implications for female inmates. By contrast, transferring females to men's prisons is less significant because transgender female prisoners are few in number, they rarely wish to transfer, and they pose less of a threat (Biggs, 2020). Dr Michael Biggs traces the progression of criteria for allocating males to women's prisons from the 1990s to the 2010s: first genital surgery, then legal sex in 2004, and finally 'gender identity' (Biggs, 2020). These changes can be explained by two distinct forces: the first was the expansion of human rights in the spheres of imprisonment and health care; the second is due to queer theory and trans activists who put sustained pressure on the government which led in 2016 to regulations which facilitated the transfer of males to the women's estate. The consequences of putting queer theory into practice are that, predictably, one male inmate (Karen White) sexually assaulted two female inmates (Biggs, 2020, p. 1).

The authoritarian Left: The case of the Labour Party

At the beginning of Labour's leadership race in 2020, the issue of trans rights rapidly rose up the political agenda. The Labour Campaign for Trans Rights: Founding Statement was launched, written by "transgender and non-binary Labour members in order to advance trans liberation through the Labour Party" (Labour Campaign for Trans Rights, 2020). Allies and sympathetic Party members were urged to sign pledges which call for individuals to

- Commit to respecting trans people as their self-declared gender;
- Accept that trans women are women, trans men are men, and non-binary people are non-binary;
- Accept that there is no material conflict between trans rights and women's rights;
- Organise and fight against transphobic organisations such as WPUK, LGB Alliance and other trans-exclusionist hate groups;
- Support the expulsion from the Labour Party of those who express bigoted, transphobic views;
- Support reform of the GRA to improve transgender rights.

All the leadership and deputy leadership candidates, including the eventual leadership winner, Keir Starmer, declared their agreement with the proposition that "trans women are women and trans men are men." But the women candidates went further and signed the pledges, including Lisa Nandy.

At an election hustings, Nandy was asked the question: "Should a rapist be placed in a women's prison if he claims to be a woman?" She replied in the affirmative, asserting that trans prisoners "should be accommodated in a prison of their choosing" (Nandy, 2020). She characterised WPUK which upholds the view that there should be sex-segregated safe spaces for women, as denying the rights of 'transwomen' to exist and causing trans people deep hurt. She alleges that WPUK "pits some women against other women," namely 'cis-women' against 'transwomen'. She was also asked about the Labour Party conference 2019 where there was a borderline-violent demonstration outside a meeting of WPUK, as discussed earlier. She refused to comment (Nandy, 2020).

In a BBC Radio 4 interview about her position on transgenderism, Nandy insisted the Party should exclude from its membership one of the co-founders of WPUK because it is "trying to do harm to other people." She also asserted, "we're a compassionate party, we believe in a compassionate society ... If you start from the position that transwomen are women ... then you don't exclude women from women-only spaces" (Nandy, 2020a). In both this interview and at the earlier campaign event, Nandy voiced a clear self-perception that she is proffering a calming position, welcoming a rational discussion about safe spaces for women. But since her stipulations for discussion contain a number of immovable conditions, namely the unequivocal acceptance that 'transwomen' *are* women, that people should be allowed to enter sex-segregated spaces according to the gender with which they identify rather than their biological sex, and that anyone even questioning these principles is transphobic, this appears to offer no opportunity for dialogue at all. She asserted that under her leadership there would be robust policies that mean women can be protected from violence in women-only spaces such as prisons or refuges but she stopped short from naming from whence the violence might come. Such a policy would be made on a case-by-case basis, she assured us, where service providers can raise an objection. This is circular reasoning: If trans women are women, then the exemptions in the *Equality Act 2010* that allow the providers of single-sex facilities to exclude trans women in some tightly controlled circumstances could only be interpreted as transphobic — as would the clause in Labour's 2019 Manifesto that promised to, "Ensure that the single-sex based exemptions contained in the *Equality Act 2010* are understood and fully enforced in service provision" (Labour Party Manifesto, 2019).

WPUK (2020b) have raised substantial concerns with the recently appointed leader, Keir Starmer, about Labour's attitude to gender critical women who believe in biological sex, and have been harassed and abused in their Labour Party branches and online by other members of the Labour Party. An earlier WPUK (2020a) complaint about the aggressive and intimidating protest at a Brighton unofficial Labour Party fringe event has been completely ignored. Moreover, none of the leadership or deputy leadership candidates supplied evidence of the scurrilous claims made in the transgender pledge or requested a meeting (WPUK, 2020b).

The seeming indifference of the Labour Party with regard to women's rights can be exemplified by an incident in 2018 when Linda Bellos, the Labour Party veteran described earlier, faced legal action in relation to comments made at a political meeting called 'We Need to Talk about the GRA'. 'Transwoman' Giuliana Kendal had been watching the live-streaming where Bellos stated she would defend herself against any 'transwoman' who threatened violence towards her. This comment was made in the context of Bellos reflecting on a previous incident. In 2017, 'transwoman' Tara Wolf, a male of 26 years of age, assaulted a 60-year-old woman named Maria MacLachlan in Hyde Park, London, where feminists had gathered to discuss the GRA reforms and were met by hostile transactivists. *The Times* journalist Janice Turner was at that meeting and witnessed the incident. Turner had asked a young activist if she was OK with men smacking women: "It's not a guy, you're a piece of s*** and I'm happy they hit her," came the reply (Turner, 2017). Wolf was in fact later convicted of assault, but unfortunately, the District Judge warned MacLachlan to refer to her assailant as "she" while giving evidence (Ward, 2018).

Kendal complained to South Yorkshire Police that, as a 'transwoman', 'she' found Bellos' alleged promised violence threatening (Two Hare Court Chambers, 2018). The police launched a full investigation, including interviewing Bellos under caution, who then faced a possible conviction for the offence of using threatening, abusive or insulting words or behaviour. Kendal was informed that the Crown Prosecution Service (CPS) had reviewed the matter at a high level and decided that there was no realistic prospect of conviction, taking into account the context in which the words were uttered and the fact that Bellos would have a defence of freedom of speech. Despite this, Kendal decided, unsuccessfully as it turned out, to bring a private prosecution against Bellos.[13]

WPUK describes the threatened legal action against Linda Bellos as part of a relentless campaign against women who speak up about reform of the GRA. This includes the intimidation of venue organisers, aggressive picketing of meetings, the assault on MacLachlan and the attempt to silence women like Bellos. These are all interferences with the democratic process about which the Labour Party Leadership remains completely silent (WPUK, 2018).

Intersectional feminism revisited

A branch of feminism now mobilises the men's rights movement (see Chapter One). Again, the example of the prison can help illustrate this. The intersectional feminist philosophers Drs Lorna Finlayson, Katherine Jenkins and Rosie Worsdale define reform of the GRA as about "what we, as a society, owe to trans people" (2018, p. 2). They state that it is "... a no brainer:

---

13 Linda Bellos was represented by the feminist barrister Gudrun Young, who successfully invited the CPS to exercise their statutory powers to take over and discontinue the prosecution on the grounds that neither the evidential sufficiency nor interests of justice test of the Code for Crown Prosecutors were met, that it was a politically motivated and vexatious prosecution, and that Giuliana Kendal was incapable of fulfilling duties as a prosecutor in a fair and impartial manner. The CPS took over the prosecution and discontinued it (Two Hare Court Chambers, 2018).

its effects for cis women will be negligible, and it will make it a little easier for people to live with dignity and respect in the gender that fits their identity" (Finlayson *et al*, 2018, p. 25). Finlayson *et al* allege that the WPUK criteria for excluding 'transwomen' from sex protected spaces such as prisons may *appear* on the surface to be "unobjectionable, common sense points which are decisive against proposals to reform the GRA" (Finlayson *et al*, 2018, p. 9). However, the problem, as they see it, is that these "purportedly feminist worries are not *just* about self-identification, but about trans inclusivity more broadly" (Finlayson *et al*, 2018, p. 7).

Finlayson *et al* thus impute an ulterior motive to gender critical women, namely the desire to exclude rather than the desire to protect. They say that what is "often presented" as merely an argument about self-identification "ends up sanctioning a politics that is both more exclusionary and more intrusive than is apparent on first sight" (Finlayson *et al*, 2018, p. 8).

They make a case for inclusion on the basis of their hypothesis that "trans women *are* different from cis men" (Finlayson *et al*, 2018, p. 13). They acknowledge that this hypothesis can't be proven and justify its lack of substantiation on the basis it is impossible to provide empirical evidence to back up their case. Despite copious evidence that men who identify as women are no *less* misogynistic and violent than other men (They Say This Never Happens, 2020; TranscrimeUK, 2020), they insist that there is no evidence for "the claim that trans women pose comparable risks to cis-men in terms of violence against women" (Finlayson *et al*, 2018, p. 14). On this erroneous premise, "they believe that including trans women in women-only spaces is by far the most practical approach to take under the current circumstances" (Finlayson *et al*, 2018, p. 14). In other words, instead of inferring it is they who are making an unprovable claim, they reverse evidential accountability and attribute it to critics of self-identification. They assert feminists are not justified in assuming that "all or some trans women share with cis men the features in virtue of which the latter pose a higher risk of violence to women" (Finlayson *et al*, 2018, p. 14).

Finlayson *et al* allege that when gender critical feminists hold that "keeping women's spaces for cis women only" as the "safest for cis women, or 'females'" this is "a tacit assumption that trans women are not ('really') women, and hence not a population which feminism needs to represent" (Finlayson *et al*, 2018, p. 15). Note that the term 'females' is put in inverted commas as if the biological category is in doubt, whereas the term 'trans women' is not. They argue that if, on the other hand

> ... trans women are thought of as a subset within 'women' ... then this just raises the question of why some women's safety should take precedence over that of others, especially when the risk allegedly posed to cis women by trans women seems to be purely theoretical — not supported by evidence — while the risk to trans women from cis men is beyond doubt (Finlayson *et al*, 2018, p. 15).

They contend that to house men who identify as women in male prisons jeopardises 'transwomen's' safety, ignoring "the well-established vulnerability of transwomen to violence at the hands of cis-men" (Finlayson *et al*, 2018, p. 17). Here we have a quintessential demonstration that the insistence that transwomen are women goes along with the sentiment that the safety of a tiny percentage of the population should trump and supersede the safety of women as a sex class. Women should just buckle down, shut up, but extend the hand of social solidarity *even if* 'transwomen' are violent within the sisterhood. Finlayson *et al* suggest that "if we think of trans women as one among many groups within the larger group 'women', then it becomes unclear how their exclusion from women's spaces could be justified *even if* there were compelling evidence that they were more prone to violence than cis women are." We should "look for other ways to respond, ways to honour bonds of solidarity rather than resorting to exclusion" (Finlayson *et al*, 2018, p. 16).

Like HMPPS, Finlayson *et al* treat White's sexual offending as a singular event, whose cause lies in the failure of prison authorities to conduct an adequate risk assessment, an error which can be mitigated in future, if adequate procedures for supervision are set in place. A convicted rapist "regardless of gender should not be held where they have unsupervised access to potential victims" (Finlayson *et al*, 2018, p. 24). Note that these authors categorise rape as sex neutral, despite the fact that firstly, under English law (*Sexual Offences Act 2003*), rape is a crime only committed by males and requires penetration by a penis, and secondly, sexual assault in the overwhelming majority of cases is perpetrated by men. Presumably, their 'sleight of hand' lies in the fact that, in order to make a case for inclusion of human beings with penises to be allowed into the female estate, there is a need to deflect attention from the fact that it is men as a sex class who rape women! Moreover, they blame the "oversights" which led to White's sexual assaults on UK austerity policies which had brought the prison system to its knees in terms of low numbers of staff (Finlayson *et al*, 2018, p. 24).

In conclusion, those committees, public bodies, politicians and intersectional feminists located within the trans human rights paradigm have elicited no concern about the general impact on female prisoners who have not been systematically monitored in any way, despite the potentially significant impacts on their sense of safety, both physical and psychological (Murray and Hunter Blackburn, 2019). These considerations are clearly exacerbated in a context in which prisoners do not have the freedom to escape, as well as a high likelihood that these women had experienced domestic and sexual abuse, and that for many abused women, a male-free space is essential. There is also no publicly available official information on how the policy change has affected female staff working with male-bodied prisoners with histories of extreme violence (Murray and Hunter Blackburn, 2019). While policy on transgender prisoners concerns the safety and well-being of two groups of prisoners — women and 'transwomen' — both regarded as vulnerable, the decision-making process has only treated the vulnerability of trans prisoners as relevant (Murray and Hunter Blackburn, 2019). According to this particular reading of ethics, since 'transwomen' not only *are* women, but according to the queer bifurcation of women into two groups, 'cis' and 'trans', they are the most vulnerable of all women, then it is only rational and morally requisite that they should be included in *all* spaces designated for *all* women to protect them from men.

These organisations are also obdurately inured to the violence directed at WPUK, much of it perpetrated by 'transwomen'. The intersectional position is that "it's no mystery why people might not only disagree but be offended or angered" (Finlayson *et al*, 2018, p. 22). And then, a disclaimer is provided: "We do not, of course, condone violence, threats or abuse." Nevertheless, "trans exclusionary feminists ... are not really justified in being either surprised or affronted when others interpret those arguments as bigoted or hateful ... the right to 'free speech' does not include a right to say ... transphobic things without anyone pointing it out (Finlayson *et al*, 2018, p. 22).

Chapter Four
The Naked Emperor

4.1 Sex Matters

Over the last 150 years women have gained significant legal rights, previously denied us on the basis of our sex (Murray and Hunter Blackburn, 2019). In 1975, the *Sex Discrimination Act* defined a woman as "a female of any age" and stated: "A person discriminates against a woman in any circumstances ... if on the ground of her sex he treats her less favourably than he treats or would treat a man." The definition of woman as an adult human female, and the recognition that biological sex is relevant to discrimination against women, were principles carried forward to the *Equality Act 2010* which set out further rights to single-sex services and spaces (Murray and Hunter Blackburn, 2019). However, despite robust evidence to show that biological sex is still extremely relevant to women's experiences of discrimination, policies that represent a profound conceptual change in our understanding about what it means to be a woman have been introduced into governance without due diligence, democratic oversight or scrutiny. Trans policy-capture demonstrates how easily systems have been influenced by the determination of single-issue, ideologically driven groups such as Stonewall, Press for Change and Gendered Intelligence.

These organisations consist of a small number of influential actors who represent an extremely small constituency but who have secured a monopoly on including queer theory into policy-making and law.

Policy experts Dr Kath Murray, Lucy Hunter Blackburn, and Lisa Mackenzie (Murray, Blackburn, Mackenzie, 2020; Murray and Hunter Blackburn, 2019) and Dr Alice Sullivan, Professor of Social Science, alert us to the way that the law and social policy, in replacing sex with 'gender identity', will have an impact on all women's lives whether they have any understanding of queer theory or have even heard of it. In particular, they draw attention to impending changes to the Scottish census, allowing individuals to tick the boxes F (female) or M (male) according to the 'gender identity' with which they identify, or of creating a third option to allow those identifying as neither male nor female to provide an alternative answer. This means that the Scottish Census authorities, who consulted trans organisations only, propose to use a different interpretation of sex than is included in current law (namely the *Equality Act 2010*). This is extremely problematic because, if implemented, it would mean that the 2021 census would have a question on 'sex', but it would not produce data on the usual legal or scientific definition of sex for the whole population. Yet the purpose of the census is to provide robust, detailed evidence in order to develop policy, plan and run public services, and allocate money to public authorities. Census data are also widely used by academics, businesses, voluntary organisations and the public.

Murray and Hunter Blackburn (2019) show that 'gender identity' lobbyists have campaigned for many years to remove sex as a protected characteristic in law. Much of it has been done quietly, behind the scenes, without public debate, due process or democratic scrutiny. Sex and 'gender identity' are entirely distinct concepts. The census, and surveys in general, need to avoid conflating them. Since at least 2008, the census authorities have been lobbied by, and have consulted with, pro-trans organisations that conflate the two, whereas groups representing women's interests have not been consulted. Nor have there been specific discussions of the consequences of moving away from collecting clear data on sex for academic researchers or public bodies which use this data (Murray and Hunter Blackburn, 2019).

Alice Sullivan demonstrates that all data collection risks being influenced by "a set of inter-locking fallacies about sex, which derive from queer theory." She identifies some of these fallacies:

- There are more than two sexes and/or sex is a spectrum;
- People with intersex conditions are a 'third sex' and/or intersex conditions are a form of gender identity;
- Sex is a (western) social construct which is arbitrarily assigned at birth;
- Non-binary individuals are neither male nor female;
- It is offensive to acknowledge the existence of biological sex. (Sullivan, 2020, p. 520).

Any questioning of these 'truths' is met by exceptional intolerance by 'gender identity' extremists, and "a remarkably successful campaign to shut down debate" (Sullivan, 2020, p. 521). Since critical voices are no longer heard, "a false 'consensus' emerges" (Sullivan, 2020, p. 522).

Academics, research organisations and policymakers need to be alert to this climate of fear and silencing in order to counter it (Sullivan, 2020). Although genuine expertise protects against policy capture, it is of grave concern that the census authorities, in carrying out a survey of whether such changes would be welcome, appear to have treated submissions from university staff with no relevant disciplinary expertise, but a clear ideological agenda, with at least equal weight to the views of population data users. As online activism among university staff and students becomes increasingly prevalent, it is important that the organisations being lobbied are able to distinguish between self-identified experts and genuine ones. Without accurate data on sex, Sullivan argues, we lose the ability to understand sex differences and to "design evidence-based policies tackling problems facing girls and boys, women and men." We also lose the ability "to gain an accurate understanding of issues facing trans people of both sexes" (Sullivan, 2020, p. 253).

Sullivan (2020) warns that a culture of silencing and policy capture by 'gender identity' lobbyists uniquely affects this aspect of data collection, shutting down critical discussion, and allowing normal measurement considerations to seem irrelevant. Since the postmodernist/queer project is explicitly anti-scientific it is vital that social statisticians understand the origins of the attempt to dismantle sex as a category in postmodernist queer theory. For queer theorists, dismantling categories is a political project. Social scientists who are interested in measuring social phenomena that are 'out there' in the real world should understand that

> ... the postmodernists who used to denigrate all quantitative research are now coming for our questionnaires. Resisting postmodernism matters for everyone who believes that the distinction between fact and fiction matters for research and policy (Sullivan, 2020, p. 523).

Philosopher Professor Kathleen Stock describes how women are now in danger of losing the legal capacity to discuss what we see as our distinctive nature and interests (Stock, 2019). The dismissal of sex as a relevant policy tool "leaves us with no adequate language to describe a politically important feature of material reality," undermines our ability to "track actual facts about sex, as it operates across various social groups, practices and discourses," as well as describing the effects of sexism and misogyny (Stock, 2019). The Office for National Statistics (ONS) figures for England and Wales show that 94% of convicted murderers and 97% of individuals prosecuted for sexual offences between 2018 and 2019 are male (ONS, 2020). Yet guidance offered by the UK Crown Prosecution Service, and apparently currently followed by UK police and the court system, advises that crimes committed by trans people are recorded in a manner consonant with the criminals' preferred self-identification. Since police forces now record crimes done by men as though they were committed by women at the request of the perpetrator, this is likely to skew the statistics for certain crimes, particularly those crimes overwhelmingly carried out by men.

Kathleen Stock points out that a practice of recording crime according to the criminals' preferred self-identification will thwart the reasonable aim of getting a clear statistical picture of certain types of crime according to sex category. In a society where sexual assaults on females by males are endemic, and given the asymmetry between male and female offending, as well as the fact that crimes such as rape that women rarely or cannot commit in the UK are now being designated as 'female', there is huge potential for crime statistics to be rendered meaningless (Stock, 2019). This change will risk corrupting what is normally a major source of research data for academics and policy-makers about sex and related matters. The result is the undermining of the capacity to combat sexism, since the lack of sex-specific data will undermine the special measures introduced to create equality of opportunity in a sexist world (Stock 2019).

Diversity and exclusion

Queer policy capture has severe consequences for the avowed ethical aspiration of liberal democracy to achieve diversity and inclusion. Stonewall's Consultancy Services and Training, and Champions Schemes for organisations, allows it, under the banner of diversity, to shape the ideas of institutions and individuals whose organisations have joined the schemes (Bailey, 2020). With regard to employers, subscribing organisations are encouraged through a Stonewall Diversity Champion scheme to 'embed' a culture of trans-inclusion and involve and engage all staff with Stonewall's values. Membership of the Champions Schemes goes beyond simply creating an inclusive environment for trans employees but is meant to create transformation in the culture and values of the subscribing organisation. With regard to children and education, for example, Stonewall has an Education Champions programme (Stonewall, 2020c), a Children and Young People's Services Champions programme (2020d) and Consultancy Services for Education and Youth Professionals (2020e).

The criminal defence barrister Allison Bailey is a casualty of the undemocratic over-reach of Stonewall, and its influence over the body politic, and the extraordinary powers it has accumulated as arbiter of who is included and who is excluded. Bailey is a black woman who describes herself as "a feminist, a lesbian, a lifelong campaigner for racial equality, and for lesbian, gay, and bisexual rights, and a survivor of child sexual abuse" (Bailey, 2020). As a lesbian, she should experience herself as an included member of the constituency Stonewall represents. She doesn't, for some of the following reasons.

Firstly, Stonewall has unilaterally and without any mandate whatsoever, "to further its lobbying ambitions," redefined homosexuality as *same-gender* attraction rather than same-sex attraction. Bailey argues this is an especially egregious betrayal of LGB people, especially women. As part of its 'diversity training' Stonewall gives lectures on the "cotton ceiling" — the term used to encourage lesbians to have sex with males who identify as women (because 'transwomen' allegedly *are* women) (Bailey, 2020). The inclusion of male-bodied people

— often with intact penises — into the class of lesbian women means that women are excoriated for bigotry and transphobia simply for being same-sex attracted. Bailey insists this is abusive, coercive and fundamentally homophobic (Bailey, 2020).

Secondly, although Stonewall's mantra is "acceptance without exception," Bailey points out it is partisan, and particularly promotes men — male people who identify as women — to the detriment of women and children. As a woman, a lesbian, a criminal defence barrister, and someone who has had extensive experience of male violence, abuse and oppression of women, Bailey insists "there should be some exceptions" (Bailey, 2020). Stonewall explicitly campaigns for the removal of the single-sex exemptions contained in the *Equality Act 2010* (see Chapter Three). Although flagged as inclusive, trans policy changes have failed women and girls, whose interests have consistently been left out. No systematic work has been carried out to consider the possible wider impacts on women to establish how the societal change has been experienced by women using services, or whether some women might be self-excluding as a result.

Thirdly, Bailey points out that gender non-conforming children and young people, who would otherwise overwhelmingly grow up to be happily LGB, are vulnerable to the 'born in the wrong body' narrative, leading to an explosion in medical and surgical procedures on healthy young bodies, especially female bodies, so as to conform to 1950s gender stereotypes.

With other LGB rights campaigners, Bailey has set up the LGB Alliance as a counterpart to Stonewall (see Chapter One).

Stonewall, in retribution, has co-ordinated with her barristers' chambers (a member of Stonewall's Diversity Champions scheme) to put her under investigation. Bailey describes this as an attempt by Stonewall to intimidate and silence her and others critical of what they regard as "its malign influence in British life: workplaces, schools, universities, the police, the judiciary, the Crown Prosecution Service, and all government departments" (Bailey, 2020). She is currently taking steps to take her case to an Employment Tribunal to show that no one should be discriminated against or victimised for campaigning for lesbian, gay and bisexual rights and that LGB people are free to organise and campaign around sexual orientation — not 'gender identity' — without apology or permission from Stonewall or anyone else (Bailey, 2020). Although the Black Lives Matter Movement is swiftly gathering momentum in the UK and globally, I note that to my knowledge, not a single intersectional feminist voice is raised against Stonewall's illegitimate attempt to oust Bailey, a black barrister, from her profession.

With regard to children and the education system, Stephanie Davies-Arai, Director of Transgender Trend, points to her grave concerns about the content of Stonewall's guidance for both primary and secondary schools (Davies-Arai, 2018). Transgender Trend was set up in 2015 as a counterpart to Stonewall (and other lobby groups) and speaks with a different voice. It provides a forum for concerned citizens, teachers and parents worried about the social and medical 'transition' of children, the introduction of 'gender identity' teaching into schools, and new policies and legislation based on subjective ideas of 'gender identity' rather than the biological reality of sex. Stephanie Davies-Arai points out that since there is no evidence that human beings possess "an internal sense of their own gender" which exists independent of both biological sex and socialisation, Stonewall's teaching materials based on queer theory should not be taught to children as fact, nor should queer theory be used as the basis of school policies. When Stonewall reframes gender dysphoria as an identity badge, it absolves schools of the responsibility to offer individualised support to each child and replaces it with a blanket politicised approach. The child is presented as a member of a political rights group, rather than as a child who may be experiencing distress and confusion and who is in need of careful and thoughtful support. Stonewall shows absolutely no concern about the increasing number of teenage girls binding their breasts, taking off-label testosterone (with irreversible effects on their bodies), and planning double mastectomies. The politicisation of gender dysphoria understands 'discrimination' against trans people — transphobia — as the singular reason for any distress a child may suffer. If psychotherapists do become involved, Stonewall insists that they are trained in 'gender identity', presumably so that the young person is not in danger of being given any other model for self-reflection (Davies-Arai, 2018; see Chapter Two for an identical approach to Stonewall's taken by Gendered Intelligence).

Trans rights activists and their supporters in the liberal media, and powerful organisations such as Stonewall, demonstrate a myopic, self-righteous normativity under the guise of diversity and inclusion. Behind a wafer-thin supposedly 'radical' anti-heteronormative posturing, their 'diversity rhetoric' results in furthering established male power and excludes the women who do not give it deference. This doesn't mean that women are not involved in this masculinist project. On the contrary, many of the main mobilisers are female as described earlier. Whittle and Stewart themselves are biologically female and did not transition until they were adult women. The men's rights movement does not neatly divide the world into opposing camps of men and women; indeed, there are notable men who are currently supporting women's resistance.[14] It means that the distilled traits of socially constructed masculinity — dominance, controlling others — are politically magnified and that the *casualties* of this illiberalism and authoritarianism embedded in social policy are women and children.

Diversity policies, saturated with a monologic view of 'gender identity', execute a masculinist trans rights political programme through the universities, the health care system,

---

14 Notable men in the UK include Dr David Bell (Consultant Psychiatrist in the Adult Department at the Tavistock and Portman NHS Foundation Trust); Johnny Best (former director of Queer Up North International Festival); Dr Michael Biggs (Associate Professor of Sociology, University of Oxford); Malcolm Clark (co-founder LGB Alliance and producer and director of science documentaries for BBC and other broadcasters); David Davies (Conservative Party MP); Dr Marcus Evans (psychoanalyst, Director Society for Evidence Based Gender Medicine); Andrew Gilligan (government policy advisor and journalist); James Kirkup (Director of the Social Market Foundation and journalist); Graham Linehan (sit-com writer); Lord Lucas (backbench Conservative Peer); Harry Miller (former police officer and co-founder of Fair Cop).

Gender Identity Development Clinics, the school system, the police and political parties in the UK. Through this politicised programme 'group think', the majority of the population — women — have a 'cis' identity foisted upon us and cries of transphobia are heard whenever a woman rejects the idea that male bodied humans are our 'sisters' (just because they say they are) and who, in the 'victimisation awards', suffer extreme oppression at our hands. That such a paradigm shift has taken place without formal scrutiny or proper monitoring far ahead of legal change, raises serious questions. The dynamics and processes which have allowed this societal change to happen for so many years, on such a scale, with so much money poured into it but so little scrutiny, deserve much closer attention, not just in order to understand the specific vulnerabilities of the historic and hard fought-for rights of women and children, but also the vulnerabilities of the democratic polity more generally (Murray and Hunter Blackburn, 2019).

4.2 The Butlerian Jihad

Powerful protests for racial and social justice are currently sweeping many countries. On the one hand, reflection on the exclusionary dynamics of race, class, sex/and gender and how one might be unwittingly complicit is needed and welcome. On the other hand, impelled self-policing for unconscious bias is simultaneously serving to intensify the moral attitudes and political commitments that for some years have been weakening norms of open debate and tolerance of difference in liberal democratic societies. An open letter to *Harper's Magazine* (2020) from writers, journalists and academics, including the famous author J.K. Rowling, says: "Censoriousness is spreading more widely in our culture: an intolerance of opposing views, a vogue for public shaming and ostracism, and the tendency to dissolve complex policy issues in a blinding moral certainty."

Adherence to queer theory forbids any discussion about sex and gender that does not restrict itself to 'gender identity', namely the sexist social construct that gives ideological effect to women's oppression. Faith in 'gender identity' is hardening into its own brand of dogma, ideological conformity and coercion. Philosopher Dan Fisher calls the imposition of queer on the culture and institutions "The Butlerian Jihad" (Fisher, 2017).

The Butlerian Jihad declares critics of queer to be the true enemies of human rights, and, as in all patriarchal systems, those who are most accused of misdemeanour and wrongdoing are women. The phenomenon of policing women is occurring in Europe, North America, Australia and elsewhere, but a few examples from the UK will have to suffice here. Let me note, however, that they will not do justice to the scale of the global misogyny we are witnessing, nor to women's indefatigable resistance.

Early in my analysis of the consequences for women and children of supplanting sex with 'gender identity' I attended a meeting in Bristol in the spring of 2018. I had been invited to give a talk based on my research for the recently published book *Transgender Children and Young People: Born In Your Own Body*. Transactivists from an organisation called Sisters Uncut physically prevented me (and the journalist Julie Bindel) from entering the conference room. We had resorted to attempting to gain entry at the back of a building up a narrow stairwell since the demonstrators, in full view of the police, had blocked the front door to what was a public community centre and had themselves stormed the building in an attempt to set off a smoke bomb and prevent the debate going ahead. I was polite to my tall, physically intimidating male-bodied masked 'sister' who forced me backwards down the stairs and called me a Nazi. I am filmed by Julie Bindel requesting to be let through and uttering the words "I wish you no harm" (YouTube, 2018). A Channel 4 documentary subsequently described me, not the protestors, as having controversial views (Channel 4, 2018)![15]

---

15 Stella O'Malley, psychotherapist, describes making the documentary 'Trans Kids: It's Time to Talk' which filmed the Bristol event as part of the film. She declares that the process, from start to finish, including the Channel 4 part, was "embroiled in dishonest, vitriolic and toxic tactics designed to prevent it" (O'Malley 2019, p. 164). She had initially hoped the film would be an open exploration of child transition and to that end she, and the director, sought preliminary discussions with those who had a stake in the issue. She was dismayed by a wall of silence. Those who refused to engage were: Maria Miller, Member of Parliament and Chair of the Women and Equality Commission that had produced the Transgender Equality Report (see Chapter Three); Dr Polly Carmichael, Director of the GIDS (see Chapter Two); Dr Helen Webberley, a private doctor who administers puberty blockers to children (now suspended by the General Medical Council for prescribing cross-sex hormones to a 12-year-old); Susie Green, CEO of Mermaids (see Chapter Two); Gendered Intelligence;

This debacle was a significant event for me. Although I was still reeling from the shock of the expulsion from the WEP and the distance it was determined to achieve between its intersectional feminist views and my gender critical views (see Chapter Three), I began (almost bodily) to fully grasp the frightening implications for women when we become non-compliant with an ideology or an article of faith that serves the patriarchy — in this instance that transwomen *are* women, that some children *are* 'born in the wrong body.'

I went on to co-found The Women's Human Rights Campaign (with Professor Sheila Jeffreys and the academic lawyer Maureen O'Hara), a global organisation launched in New York in the spring of 2019 (Women's Declaration, 2019). We have set out a number of principles that women can use to counteract the Yogyakarta Principles (described earlier in Chapter Three) which were largely written by people whose identities fall under the trans umbrella. The Women's Declaration asserts principles which re-affirm women's sex-based rights and demonstrates the discrimination against women and girls that results from 'gender identity.' These sex-based principles are currently discussed by women on regular Webinars across the globe and are an aid to

---

Stonewall; Paris Lees, a journalist and trans rights activist (see Prologue); Owen Jones, *Guardian* journalist with forthright affirmative views on trans; Alex Bertie, a usually very media forthcoming trans vlogger; Lily Madigan, an assertive male-to-female trans campaigner and Women's Spokesperson for the Labour Party (described earlier in Chapter Three), and Member of Parliament Justine Greening, a driving force behind plans for LGBT-inclusive sex education in the UK and for reform of the GRA (O'Malley, 2019).

resisting 'gender identity' policy capture in women's different countries.

In 2019, a petition to remove Michele Moore, Professor of Social Justice, as editor-in-chief of the journal *Disability & Society* was mounted and sent to Taylor & Francis, the journal's publisher. The petition had 800 signatures, and four editors resigned in protest over Moore's alleged transphobia because of her concerns about medically transitioning children and young people (Yeomans, 2019). The signatories called "in the strongest possible terms" for the publishers to remove her from her post and for the editorial board to publicly condemn "anti-transgender bigotry." They asked the Board to "affirm the inherent worth of the transgender and gender nonconforming members of the disability community specifically, and the lives of transgender and gender nonconforming people broadly" (Letter to *Disability & Society* Editorial Board, 2019). "In academia, we support conscientious, informed argumentation, but the lives and dignity of transgender people are not up for debate," they said. "Moore's public trans-antagonism risks making *Disability & Society* complicit in epistemic violence and active harm" (Letter to *Disability & Society* Editorial Board, 2019). Fortunately, the publishers did not force Moore to stand down, and after the bullying eventually subsided (although it rumbles beneath the surface and occasionally manifests itself elsewhere in her academic life), the journal has recovered its prestige and world-leading status.

Universities are increasingly affirming Gendered Intelligence's doctrine on 'gender identity' as officially established truth, incorporating it into university diversity and inclusion policy and promulgating it through Equality and Diversity Units (Biggs, 2018c). Gendered Intelligence's course on 'Trans Awareness' has been repeated in dozens of universities across the UK. It plays a key role in training academic staff, administrators, and counsellors for students; students who question their own identity are directed to it as resource. Policy thus goes far beyond what is required by the *Equality Act*, which rightly forbids discrimination on the grounds of gender reassignment (Biggs, 2018c). Biggs points out that the establishment of an official doctrine on 'gender identity' is an unprecedented threat to academic freedom since universities grant one particular group extraordinary power to control intellectual discourse. Scholars who question the orthodoxies of queer theory are subjected to vicious harassment and intimidation (Biggs, 2018c).

An academic who wishes to remain anonymous exemplifies the authoritarianism of Gendered Intelligence when criticism of its alleged new intelligent paradigm of thought about gender is comparable to an old reactionary one, only rebranded. The academic attended a trans awareness workshop delivered by Gendered Intelligence at a prestigious, Russell Group, university. The university had imposed a code of conduct — written by Gendered Intelligence — on those attending the workshop, requiring them to "refrain from using language or putting forward views intended to undermine the validity of trans and gender diverse identities" (A Gender Critical Woman, 2020). This code of conduct is itself in contravention of the legal obligation of universities to ensure freedom of speech for students, employees and visiting speakers. A very serious set of allegations was made by Gendered Intelligence against this particular gender critical feminist and she was subjected to a disciplinary process involving a two-hour-long investigation interview and two formal hearings within her own university. Eventually, she was cleared of any wrongdoing but believes she had a narrow escape from "The Trans Cult Bullies" (A Gender Critical Woman, 2020).

Academics face campaigns of vexatious complaints, no-platforming, and even threats of violence for simply asserting the reality and social salience of sex, especially when they do so from a feminist perspective (Sullivan, 2020). This has a "wider chilling effect" because "normal open and rigorous discourse" is effectively becoming suspended in universities (Sullivan, 2020, p. 522). Many feminist academics have been 'no-platformed' for holding gender critical views following complaints by their own students or resulting from presentations at academic conferences, including me (Bannerman, 2017b), Professor Kathleen Stock (Turner, 2020), Professor Selina Todd (Turner, 2020a), Professor Rosa Freedman (Griffiths, 2018) and Professor Alice Sullivan (Sullivan, 2020).

The intersectional feminist Sara Ahmed who works "at the intersection of feminist, queer and race studies" defends 'no debate' and no-platforming of feminists critical of 'gender identity' (Ahmed, 2015). She says the term TERF is not a slur: "it is a pretty fair and mild description of some feminists who aim to exclude trans people from feminism" (Ahmed, 2015). She assures us that applying the epithet TERF is "not the same kind of speech act as misgendering a trans woman" — presumably she means for example, referring to my masked, male-bodied 'sisters' as male — an act Ahmed "would describe as an intentional act of elimination" (Ahmed, 2015). In Ahmed's frame of reference, my description of the aggression directed at me and others at Bristol where I do not accede my assailant was female is "to cause violence against trans people ... [and is] an incitement to violence" (Ahmed, 2015). So, here is the crux of the matter — anything other than complete acquiescence to the mantra 'transwomen *are* women' has become an act of human erasure.

> Transphobia and anti-trans statements should not be treated as *just another viewpoint* that we should be free to express at a happy diversity table. *There cannot be a dialogue when some at the table are in effect or intent arguing for the elimination of others at the table.* When you have 'dialogue or debate' ... then 'dialogue and debate' becomes another technique of elimination (Ahmed, 2015).

In Ahmed's judgement, as in the moral judgement of Finlayson *et al* (2018), the "anger and rage" of the female identified male is a justifiable defence mechanism to my murderous thought crime (Ahmed, 2015).

In March 2019, Maya Forstater, an independent researcher, writer and advisor working on the business of sustainable development, lost her job at the Centre for Global Development. She had written and tweeted about her belief in biological sex and her concern about the reform of the *Gender Recognition Act* (Forstater, 2020). She took her employer to an Employment Tribunal on the grounds of their discrimination against her because of her beliefs. She lost her case, a judgment that effectively removes women's rights to freedom of belief and speech. Forstater says this gives judicial licence for women (and men) who speak up for objective truth and clear debate to be subject to aggression, bullying, no platforming and economic punishment (Forstater, 2020).

J.K. Rowling gave support on social media to Forstater's case which brought her story to international attention, sparking thousands of online, media and kitchen table conversations. Forstater has continued to voice her views, and to fight on in terms of writing and political involvement, because she did not want her story to be a "cautionary tale about the high cost to women of having the courage to speak up, but instead to try to make it a win for freedom of thought, belief and expression, and for the heart and soul of the institutions that underpin an open society" (Forstater, 2020).

J.K. Rowling has now written a long, thoughtful essay setting out her own gender critical views, namely that supporting trans rights is not incompatible with a belief that biological sex is both real and critical to women's rights (Rowling, 2020). In doing so, she wholly affirms the rights of adults to identify as they wish and is sympathetic. However, in speaking up about the importance of sex she says she has been paying the price ever since she voiced her support for Maya Forstater. "I was transphobic, I was a cunt, a bitch, a TERF, I deserved cancelling, punching and death" (Rowling, 2020). Of all the logical inconsistencies that have emerged from transactivists' proclamations, I suggest none, surely, could demonstrate more clearly the legitimacy of women's claims about the violence of militant transactivism: on the one hand, biological sex is allegedly of no significance and it is an act of violence or an abuse of human rights for women to suggest it is; on the other hand, the female body was immediately targeted in 'knee-jerk', ageist, misogynistic tropes of revulsion directed *ad nauseum* on social media, at Rowling. As an example, I relay the words of the following tweeter, and in doing so I'm temporarily mindful of Ahmed's injunction not to commit violence by 'mis-gendering'. The tweeter offers 'her' "big fat trans cock" in the hopes Rowling will "choke" on it (Screenshots, 2020).

Rowling has been denounced by our most allegedly open-minded liberal elite, or, as journalist Janice Turner describes them, "every mediocre child star she enriched ... and LGBT bodies she generously endowed" (Turner, 2020a). She nevertheless stands firm, continuing to display courage and humanity. "The trans activists, who post pornography on her timeline ... are livid about She Who Cannot Be Cancelled" (Turner, 2020a). Rowling points out that political parties, in seeking to appease the loudest voices in this debate, ignore women's concerns at their peril. In the UK, women are reaching out to each other across party lines, concerned about the erosion of our hard-won rights and widespread intimidation. The supreme irony, Rowling suggests, is that "the attempt to silence women with the word 'TERF' may have pushed more young women towards radical feminism than the movement's seen in decades" (Rowling, 2020).

The Member of Scottish Parliament, Joanna Cherry, describes the misogynist terms of abuse, in particular TERF and the threats of violence which accompany it, which are frequently hurled at female gender critical politicians, impeding the democratic process through the real fear they generate. Popular memes often involve guns pointed at 'TERFS'. Direct threats of violence and rape are not uncommon (Cherry, 2019). Women who speak out are routinely insulted on social media in the following ways: "All TERFs deserve to be shot in the head"; "TERFs Can Choke on my Girl Dick"; "Enjoy my lady dick in your mouth Cuntwipe"; 'I'm not into mass murder but I'll commit TERF genocide if I have to" (Peak Trans, 2019).

Finally, Transgender Trend has been subject on many occasions to attempts by Stonewall to silence its voice. In particular Stonewall makes defamatory unsubstantiated allegations (Davies-Arai, 2019). Stonewall has accused Transgender Trend of being "anti-trans," of believing that "trans people don't exist" and of being opposed to "LGBT inclusive education" (Davies-Arai, 2019). Defamation proceedings began in February 2018 as a response to Transgender Trend having published educational packs for schools which contain an alternative approach based on sex and gender, not 'gender identity'. Not only did Stonewall write to schools and education authorities to advise head teachers/teachers to immediately "bin" or "shred" the material (Davies-Arai, 2019); it also made a public statement on its website:

> The 'schools resource pack' produced by Transgender Trend is … so dangerous. Masquerading as professional, 'evidence-based' advice

for schools on how to 'support trans and gender nonconforming young people', the pack in fact provides the reverse. It is a deeply damaging document ... (Stonewall, 2019).

4.3 The Transgender Empire

Most people think the 'transgender' or 'gender identity' movements are about accommodating people with a debilitating condition. But they are actually an *industry* that creates medical identities out of sex, while simultaneously mounting active campaigns to deconstruct sexual dimorphism within the law. Transgenderism is a multi-billion dollar industry, disguised as a civil rights movement, or what the journalist Jennifer Bilek describes as "big business dressed up in civil rights clothes" (Bilek, 2018a). It constructs medical identities that harm children and steals funding and focus from women's authentic civil rights (Bilek, 2020). To follow the money, Bilek takes us to the root of the 'gender identity' industry where she found that exceedingly rich, white men with enormous cultural influence are funding the transgender lobby and various transgender organisations: Jennifer Pritzker, Jon Stryker, and George Soros (Bilek, 2018).

'The Gender Industrial Complex'

Michael Biggs describes 'The Gender Industrial Complex' as receiving lucrative sponsorship from pharmaceutical companies and medical providers (Biggs, 2018b). He, like Bilek (2018), points out that three American billionaires have bankrolled the transgender movement on a global scale. The Open Societies Foundations (OSF), funded by George Soros, has spent three million dollars between 2011 and 2013 on trans issues to promote the transgender movement which made it the top funder, followed by Stryker's Arcus Foundation and Pritzker's Tawani Foundation (Open Societies Foundations 2020; Bilek, 2018; Biggs, 2018b). To illustrate the difference that money can make, Biggs asks us to consider the commemoration of the victims of violence. The OSF gave US$500,000 to Transgender Europe in the past two years. Transgender Europe also received one million dollars from the Arcus Foundation from 2010 to 2017. The organisation's projects include the Transgender Day of Remembrance, which is underpinned by a comprehensive database of victims throughout the world, Trans Murder Monitoring. This database counted 325 trans victims of violence from October 2016 to September 2017 (Trans Respect Rather Than Transphobia Worldwide, 2017). The great majority of these occurred in Central and South America. There were only three in Western Europe, and thankfully none in the United Kingdom. Surprisingly, perhaps, the Transgender Day of Remembrance was widely observed in Britain in November 2017. In many universities, for example, candles were lit for each of the victims, the transgender flag was raised, speakers were invited, and services held (Biggs, 2018b).

I can testify to this student commemoration of the Transgender Day of Remembrance with an example from my own experience. I had been invited to the University of Bristol by the University Free Speech Society in November 2018 to give a lecture on the curtailment of free speech in the academy, giving the example of the incipient erasure in universities of any other than an affirmative view of 'gender identity'. Trans activist students interrupted my talk, taking over the lecture theatre and attempted to read out all the names of those murdered before eventually being removed by the security guards who had been specifically commissioned to protect me that evening (Ross, 2017).

As Michael Biggs points out, while no transgender person was murdered in the United Kingdom in 2017, 138 women were killed by men, including murders where a man was the principal suspect (Smith, 2018). These data were compiled by Karen Ingala Smith, who receives no funding for her work. She started recording women's deaths in 2009, under the rubric of Counting Dead Women. This was developed into the Femicide Census — in partnership with Women's Aid — with minimal funding and pro-bono support from two legal firms (Femicide Census, 2016). Despite her diligent research over many years, this has left barely a trace in British universities. More than a hundred women are murdered each year in the United Kingdom at the hands of males, but no day has been set aside to commemorate their deaths. Transgender murders are exceedingly rare — eight in the past decade (Trans Crime UK, 2017) — and yet they have an institutionalised day of remembrance. Even if we consider the homicide rate rather than the number of homicides, Nicola Williams demonstrates that transgender people are no more likely to become victims than are women (Fairplay for Women, 2017a). The prominence of transgender victims, compared to the virtual invisibility of female victims, is partly explained by the amount of resources devoted to compiling evidence and promoting commemoration. Thus, as Biggs demonstrates, funding from large American charities like OSF — along with the Arcus and Tawani Foundations — shapes the political climate in Britain and around the world (Biggs, 2018b).

Transgenderism is a capitalist enterprise driven by the pharmaceutical industry (Bilek, 2018). Over the past decade, there has been an explosion in transgender medical infrastructure across the United States and world to 'treat' transgender people. The massive medical and technological infrastructure expansion for a tiny (but growing) fraction of the population, along with the money being funnelled into the transgender project by those heavily invested in the medical and technology industries, means that doctors are being trained in all manner of surgeries related to transgender individuals, including phalloplasty, vaginoplasty, facial feminisation surgery, urethral procedures, and more. Manufacturing puberty blockers for children and young people is another growing and extremely lucrative market. With the medical infrastructure being built, doctors being trained for various surgeries, clinics opening at speed, and the media celebrating it, transgenderism is poised for further growth (Bilek, 2018).

In the UK, lobby organisations have become businesses that receive a substantial percentage of their funding from the UK Government or other statutory bodies (see Stonewall, 2020b). Michael Biggs tells us that Gendered Intelligence started as a company with a grant of £50,000 from the Equality and Human Rights Commission (EHRC). Now most of its revenue comes from selling training to the public sector, including universities, boosted by monies from BBC Children in Need (Biggs, 2018c). Davies-Arai (2019) informs us that Stonewall is the most powerful and influential LGBT organisation in the UK with an income of £8.7 million in 2018 including a £233,673 grant from the Department for Education. Gary Powell, Conservative Party Councillor and erstwhile gay rights activist, says that although Stonewall began as a worthy institution fighting for homosexual rights, "its cash registers have become frenetic" (Powell, 2020). In 2018, its most senior employee earned a six-figure salary, and it received £610,000 in grant income from Government sources, with a fee income of £2,731,000 that included payments from local authorities for its workplace Diversity Champions and Secondary Schools Champions programmes (Powell, 2020). In 2015, Stonewall and similar western charities "bolted trans rights on to their LGB campaigns, even though gender identity has nothing to do with sexual orientation." With legal equality for LGB people successfully achieved in the west, Powell argues these charities needed new victims and causes to maintain their cashflow. He points out that "'Gender identity' ideology was ideal: between 2014 and 2018, Stonewall's turnover increased by 61 per cent" (Powell, 2020).

In summary, the money invested by rich men, governments, technology and pharmaceutical corporations effectively normalises transgenderism as a lifestyle choice. The micro-politics and the macro-politics of 'identity' interact to form one of the most misogynistic expressions of patriarchy in recent times under the guise of equality, diversity and inclusion. Transgenderism is positioned as a social justice movement, a medical condition, and as a minority rights issue needing protection from our political structures. It intersects at every juncture of the global marketplace and is so indelibly tied to the capitalist marketplace and celebrity culture that it is used to sell fashion, makeup, hormones, surgery, films, TV series, mental health treatments, and women's underwear, while concurrently being invested in by billionaire philanthropists, the technology and pharmaceutical industries, major corporations, and banks (Bilek, 2018a).

Big business dressed in civil rights clothes

Although the state prosecuting authority in the UK — the Crown Prosecution Service (CPS) — is tasked with being objective and impartial, it is not independent with regard to transgender issues. The CPS is a Stonewall Diversity Champion and it is thus publicly affiliated with an unelected, unaccountable, political lobbying group. Stonewall not only campaigns for removal of the provision for single-sex services in the *Gender Recognition*

Act 2004, it seeks societal reform through influencing the culture and values of its partner organisations.

That the CPS is publicly aligned with advancing of Stonewall's cause is exemplified by its policy and guidance on "transphobic hate crime" (Crown Prosecution Service, 2020). The definitions of 'trans', 'gender identity', 'gender reassignment' and 'transphobia' that are adopted by the CPS throughout its legal guidance on 'hate crime' bears close resemblance to those advocated by Stonewall (Crown Prosecution Service, 2020a). The CPS (2020) defines "hate crime" as

> ... a range of criminal behaviours where the perpetrator is motivated by hostility or demonstrates hostility towards the victim's disability, race, religion, sexual orientation or transgender identity. These aspects of a person's identity are known as 'protected characteristics'. A hate crime can include verbal abuse, intimidation, threats, harassment, assault and bullying, as well as damage to property.

Since 'transgender identity' is not a protected characteristic of the *Equality Act 2010*, the CPS can clearly be seen to be incorporating into their legal guidance Stonewall's stated aim of going above and beyond the law as it stands to render 'transgender identity' or 'gender identity' a protected characteristic. Correspondingly, there is no provision for 'sex' being included as a relevant characteristic for hate crime purposes, despite sex being included as a protected characteristic under the *Equality Act 2010*. The removal of sex as a protected characteristic by the CPS is in line with Stonewall's stated political aims. This is a significant omission by the CPS given that most violent and sexual crimes against women are perpetrated by biological males and could be deemed to be motivated by hostility based on the fact of women's biological sex. Arguably, the CPS — in treating gender but not sex as protected characteristic — is itself in breach of the *Equality Act 2010* which imposes a duty upon it not to discriminate against women.

The CPS (2020a) states that it and the police have agreed to the following definition for identifying and flagging hate crimes:

> Any criminal offence *which is perceived by the victim or any other person,* to be motivated by hostility or prejudice ... There is no legal definition of hostility so we use the everyday understanding of the word which includes ill-will, spite, contempt, prejudice, unfriendliness, antagonism, resentment and dislike (my emphasis).

As we saw earlier, the following have been deemed 'hateful' or 'transphobic' by those in the trans community (and their supporters): the statement 'only women have periods'; the female sign on packaging for sanitary towels; a refusal to allow an intact biological male to use a women's changing room; objection to a biological male sex offender who identifies as a woman being housed in a women's prison; the statement 'only women give birth'; the statement 'only women have vaginas'; a refusal to use third-person (or any other) pronouns an individual wishes you to use.

Although the CPS is obligated to bring criminal prosecutions and acts to enforce the law *as it stands,* CPS policy and guidance have the effect of potentially criminalising behaviour or speech which would otherwise not constitute a criminal offence. The subjective definition of a hate crime, based upon a person's perception of hostility, combined with the Stonewall definition of transphobia (arguably accepted wholesale by the CPS in its guidance), potentially leads to a situation in which a woman is guilty of committing a criminal offence if, for example, in a single-sex changing room or as a refuge worker, she refuses to accept a 'transwoman' (which Stonewall defines as meaning even a 'cross-dresser'). The adoption by the CPS of Stonewall's definitions into their policy and guidance creates a real risk that the expression of gender-critical opinions would be investigated as a transphobic crime.[16] The CPS policy and guidance actively encourages the pro-active investigation of such 'crimes' and the early 'flagging' of incidents as transphobic.[17]

---

16 I gave a paper at the UK launch of the Declaration on Women's Sex-based Rights in Leeds (Brunskell-Evans, 2019b). I was reported to the West Yorkshire Police for 'hate speech' by the 'transwoman' Natasha Handley, a trainer for Trans Leeds, an organisation which trains MPs, NHS, and the Prison Service in the Leeds area (see Handley, 2019). The West Yorkshire Police did not eventually charge me.

17 The first expression of opinion which was 'criminalised' by the police and the CPS is the following case (Manning and Walsh, 2019). Helen Islan, a Mermaids employee who frequently campaigned anonymously for transgendering children on Twitter, alleged that Amanda Yardley, a gender critical accountant, had tweeted a message linking her name to her Twitter handle and was guilty of harassing her by potentially exposing her and her transgender child to bullying and abuse. Yardley's defence was freedom of speech and that all information had been placed in the public domain by Islan herself. The CPS charged Yardley as having committed a 'transgender hate crime' and applied for reporting restrictions to protect Islan and send a message to victims of future 'transgender hate crime' that the courts would protect them by granting anonymity. The District Judge ruled that there was insufficient evidence to demonstrate 'hate speech' and the case should not have been brought (Manning and Walsh, 2019).

To summarise, the CPS, by virtue of its association with Stonewall, has assumed an ideological position on transgender matters that is not in accordance with its stated objectives to be impartial, independent and non-political. As a Stonewall Champion, it has aligned itself with a pressure group on a matter of significant national controversy, namely the issue of conflict of transgender rights and the rights of biological women. The fact that these controversial concepts and definitions have been imported by the CPS into formal policy and guidance on the very definitions of what constitutes a 'hate crime' is a matter of significant concern not only for women but for the health of liberal democracy.

In 2018, I had a disconcerting experience at a round table discussion about the updating of the *Gender Recognition Act* at the Equality and Human Rights Commission (EHRC). The EHRC is also in charge of interpreting the *Equality Act*, and it is also a Stonewall Diversity Champion. I was faced with a seemingly unmoveable conviction that the moral right was on the trans 'side'. The EHRC legal representative quite clearly saw the issue through the principle that human rights are universal, interdependent, indivisible and interrelated, as the Yogyakarta Principles assert, and that since a person's personal 'gender identity' — according to these Principles — is integral to dignity and humanity, then non-inclusion in sex-segregated spaces is tantamount to discrimination.

My own contribution to the discussion concerned women's refuges. The risk-assessment strategies recommended for refuge workers to protect women from a 'transwoman' with mal-intent seemed to me at best naïve and wholly unworkable. Many years ago, I worked in a women's refuge in London. When the doorbell rang we did not carry out an assessment of risk to others of the woman escaping from violence or 'vet' her, but immediately allowed her safe entry. Once admitted, the woman shares one intimate space with other women who *de facto* have recent experience of male violence and, as I argue with prisons, the women have the right not to have to negotiate their safe space with men who are strangers. My contribution was stonily ignored. As J.K. Rowling points out, when those from the allegedly progressive Left "demand that we give up our hard won sex-based rights, they align themselves squarely with men's rights activists ... female trauma is white noise, an irrelevance, or else exaggerated or invented" (Rowling, 2020a).

In the ethical universe of the EHRC, the organisation tasked with promoting and upholding equality and human rights ideals and laws across Britain, unless women acknowledge and accept sharing intimate spaces with men who identify as women (namely with the cross-dressers, transvestites and anyone else under the canopy of the Stonewall trans umbrella who may not conform to traditional gender roles), unless women ignore what is happening to women's sports, crime statistics, medical statistics, sex equity in the workplace, women's safety in prisons and refuges, and the abomination of medical experiments on healthy children, a moral, discriminatory mistake of the first order has been made. If trans women *are* women, there is no basis for excluding anyone who identifies as a woman from women-only spaces. To exclude a subset of the category of women would be to discriminate against that subset and would clearly be to practice a form of social apartheid that we should all condemn (Murray and Hunter Blackburn, 2019).

When a 'transwoman' requires liberal democratic society to accept that he has a woman's 'soul', has had it since he emerged from his mother's womb or even before, and consequently has to share all spaces designated for women, he is helped in exercising this illiberal, coercive power through a constellation of democratic institutions, forces and discourses. The mundane statement that people in possession of penises are not women is now so inflammatory that when it is uttered, human rights organisations are ready to dismiss this expression of fact as bigotry, and mechanisms are set in place such that the police and legal system can silence or punish this 'hate speech'. Institutions whose purpose is to defend human rights now interpret truth speech as hate speech, and oppression of women as ethics.

Political and institutional leaders, including those in the media, not only effectively help police the boundaries of per-ceived transgressions of speech according to the parameters set down by powerful organisations such as Stonewall and Gendered Intelligence, but also police ethical credentials. In the UK, health care workers proudly sport their allegiance to LGBT rights in hospitals up and down the land, including the Tavistock and Portman, by wearing declarative trans-rainbow badges. The police force whose statutory remit is to be apolitical and which, in an age of austerity, is struggling to have sufficient resources to fulfil its safeguarding responsibilities, spends thousands every year on Stonewall subscriptions (Goodenough, 2020). Women and children have already paid and are continuing to pay the price for this 'group think' through the greater risk aversion among medics, teachers, academics, lawyers and politicians who, observing the consequences of speaking out, fear for their reputations and livelihoods if they depart from the alleged consensus, or even have insufficient zeal in fulsome agreement with the quasi-religious doctrine that 'transwomen' *are* women.

Reform of the *Gender Recognition Act* (GRA)

The potential for authoritarianism and illiberalism has been creeping into all our institutions and may get more extreme if not stayed by concerted resistance. In the previous five years, women — bereft of or even denied institutional support and safeguarding by political leaders — have worked assiduously and at great personal cost to alert the public to the dangers of the GRA reforms. In doing so they have displayed great courage in the face of ostracism, risk to employment and reputation, and violence.

I have recently begun to notice a change 'in the air' — something akin to sensing the spring after a cold, frozen long UK winter — that our concerns might be taken seriously by government. Liz Truss, the newly elected Conservative Government Minister for Women and Equalities, has recently set out her approach and priorities (Truss, 2020). In contrast to the Women's Equality Select Committee 2015 led by Maria Miller, which took *no* account of the GRA's impact on women, Truss assured the current Women and Equalities Select Committee that a lot of work has been carried out internally by government to make sure it is in a position to appropriately respond to the consultation in summer 2020. She promises that three very important principles will be put in place: the protection of single-sex spaces; transgender adults will be free to live their lives as they wish without fear of persecution, whilst proper checks and balances in the system will be maintained; and under 18s will be protected from decisions they could make that are irreversible in the future (Truss, 2020).

In a response to the possible abandonment of GRA reform, Gendered Intelligence performed a *volte-face* about the significance of self-identification. Jay Stewart, the Director, has spent the last five years with a finger in nearly every political pie pushing for legal change and the removal of single-sex exemptions. Gendered Intelligence now says: "the bigger issues facing trans communities — discrimination, lack of access to robust healthcare, housing — are of more acute urgency than any potential reform to the GRA ... [and] ... inclusion in single-sex spaces" (Gendered Intelligence, 2020c). Dare we hope that the men's rights movement is now, finally, in retreat?

Conclusion

Since the way to defeat bad ideas is by exposure, argument, and persuasion, I hope this book contributes to making transparent the illiberalism smuggled into liberal democracies via the Trojan Horse named Queer Theory. In 2004, the creation of the GRA signified a nodal point in the UK around which the trans empire has been able to expand its territory. It was at this historical juncture that inner 'identity' was established as the 'true' primary marker of sex, since male or female genitals were not deemed determinative. A trans affirmative empire has thenceforth, by stealth and by utter conviction and determination, as well as by vast funding, relentlessly campaigned to erase any significance to the two morphologically distinct sexes. The queer deconstruction of sex, now instituted in the academy as well as the mainstream, means the empire has spread through the national body politic — medicine and the law, in conjunction with transactivism, government and social policy, public institutions and Big Pharma — have *en masse* helped sideline biological reality to the cost of women and children — and to the benefit of men.

In the twenty-first century, transgenderism, wearing a liberal democratic facemask, is patriarchy emblazoned in imperial form. The claim, incomprehensible in its breadth twenty years ago, that men who identify as women *are* women, even though there is no scientific evidence (neuroscientific or otherwise) that an unambiguously biological male can be female, is now so normalised it is successfully embedded as *fact* in the public consciousness. Indeed, adherence to this non-fact is seen as emblematic of an inclusive, progressive democratic society. For centuries, women have been silenced almost entirely (in the family, in the courts, and in politics) through social ostracism or the threat of violence if they had the temerity to point to politicised inequalities between the sexes. In time-honoured tradition, but with a chilling twenty-first century twist, when feminists point to the patriarchal basis of transgender ideology, we are alleged to be extremists for not allowing men's interests to control the current political narrative.

The transgender movement shift shapes by wearing a cloak of progressivism, human rights, equality, diversity and inclusion. It is particularly dangerous since it hides its authoritarianism in plain sight. Perhaps one day society will look back and wonder how, a century after women were 'allowed' to get the vote, women and men were prepared to vilify, exclude and gag by any means possible the women who saw through the pomp and stood aside from the baying, frightened crowd to declare: "The Emperor has no clothes."

Epilogue

In the late autumn of 2019, I found myself on a cold and blustery night in a church hall in Manchester. It was the inaugural event of the Detransition Advocacy Network founded by Charlie Evans, and I wasn't going to miss it for the world. Evans, a formerly trans-identified British woman, had gone public some months earlier with her decision, aged 27, to detransition (Evans, 2019). She was subsequently contacted by many others in their early twenties who were also seeking to desist from identifying as male. In a hostile environment in which detransitioners are seen as traitors or "collateral damage for the greater good," she founded the Detransition Advocacy Network to give such young women a voice and support (Evans, 2019).

The moment the questions and answers began, there was an explosive cry from somewhere in the audience. For a split second I thought a transactivist was in our midst and I braced myself for the aggression about to break out (my usual experience nowadays whenever women take the liberty of talking about our own bodies!). But this time the shout came from a sympathetic man, audibly shaken and aghast. What had he heard?

Charlie Evans is a classic example of the kinds of girls/young women who self-identify as male and who present at gender clinics (see Chapter Two). She says: "At 17 I was tightly binding my chest, and had shaved my hair, adamant that I was not a girl.

159

I knew I was a boy, because I hated the way my chest attracted attention, I hated my period … I loved cars, mud, boxing and girls" (Evans, 2019). Trans ideology tells people "everyone feels their gender," and since she didn't "feel like a girl" Evans concluded that she "must be a boy." She tells us she had "been indoctrinated into the idea that girls and boys feel certain ways and if they don't, they might be the opposite sex trapped in the wrong body." She met "all the diagnostic criteria": "a strong rejection of typically feminine traits and clothes … a mainly male friendship group" and "a desire to be treated as a boy." All the health care practitioners Evans had seen were affirming, and not one of them encouraged the idea that it was OK to be gender non-conforming. She says: "Friends and healthcare practitioners alike 'affirmed' my gender. Yes, you are a boy."

The hall was packed with perhaps 200 (or more) people, and a somewhat electric atmosphere pervaded. I was extremely aware that just two or three rows behind me sat Dr Stuart Lorimer, a UK consultant psychiatrist and specialist gender clinician, who works full-time in the NHS (at the Charing Cross Gender Identity Clinic for adults in London), as well as privately. Lorimer is notorious for his relaxed affirmation of any young person (between 17 and 25) who self-identifies as the other sex, his willingness to prescribe hormone treatment for those with the money to pay, and his commitment to the idea that transgender identification is not a psychiatric/psychological condition. He says that long waiting lists have "always been a regrettable part of gender medicine and, as numbers of transitioners have increased globally, all services have struggled under sheer weight of numbers" (Lorimer, 2017). He describes his "private service" as "friendly, accessible, tailored to individual needs." He insists the private sector is freer of the constraints of state subsidised healthcare (such as the GIDS) where some gatekeeping for the sake of sparing the public purse is necessary. In contrast, private care is "arguably 'purer'" (Lorimer, 2017).

At the Network's meeting, there were two panels: The first panel comprised four psychotherapists, one of whom had once worked at the GIDS, and one of whom was Dr David Bell, a current Tavistock employee (see Chapter Two). All expressed criticism of the affirmative approach. The second panel comprised five detransitioning young women. One of the panellists, a German woman called Olivia, bluntly told us: "I regret all of it" (Detransition Advocacy Network, 2019). The desire to transition, like an earlier episode of anorexia, was a way for her to escape her bodily "reality." She compares her body dysmorphia with her anorexia, both of which involved hatred of her female body. However, two completely different approaches were taken by her family and the medical profession. At 16 years old, nobody, she gratefully told us, accepted her 'inner truth' that she was in fact grossly overweight. Later, her fantasy was to have a body as close to that of a male as possible. "But nobody told me not to get castrated." By 21, she had a double mastectomy, a hysterectomy and removal of her ovaries (Detransition Advocacy Network, 2019).

Olivia has now realised the problem was not in her as an individual, but in society. She asked: "What are surgeons doing calling this ... gender affirming health care?" "These surgeons are perpetrators and should be in prison for doing this ... I woke up from the hysterectomy and they immediately gave me a leaflet for the phalloplasty clinic." "The surgeons give invasive surgeries ... mastectomies are brutal, and we are not expected to mourn our body parts." Medical intervention "does not make you less female ... It's not a sex change, it's castration." "I am a woman even though I have been castrated ... Only women have hysterectomies and only women will live with the consequences ... I now want to live with reality" (Detransition Advocacy Network, 2019).

On hearing Olivia's experience and that of the other panel-lists, the man in the audience blurted out an unmediated, unselfconscious response. He explained he had been 'dragged' to this meeting by his wife when he should have been out earning his living, taxi-driving. He was unconstrained by the fear of appearing bigoted, having never been exposed to the LGBT social justice discourse shared with many gender clinicians. He heard for the first time that children were being groomed by a thicket of online video resources that instruct them how to get past whatever nominal clinical gatekeeping they may encounter in Gender Identity Development Services. He learned that, as in actual cults, young people are encouraged to believe that their entire gamut of personal problems can be solved so long as they embrace one overarching trans dogma. He had discovered to his horror that, in twenty-first century Europe, North America and Australia, young women are being irrevocably sterilised whilst they are immature, still developing emotionally and psychologically. As a father, he couldn't believe that no one, neither her parents nor her clinicians, nor the state, had sought to protect Olivia from herself.

As soon as the meeting drew to a close, I observed Dr Lorimer, ashen faced, speed out of the hall and disappear into the night. He may have had a very pressing further engagement and a train to catch. He may not have been feeling well. He may, as I suspect, have been petrified that a detransitioner might accost him that evening, not as a saviour (as he imagines himself to be), but as a criminal. He may have been fearful that potential lawsuits might come his way in the next few years when young women like Olivia want to reclaim their ravaged female bodies and hold to account those professionals who 'rubber stamped' their trans claims and led them down the path of transition.

References

4thWaveNow (2015) 'The 41% trans suicide attempt rate: A tale of flawed data and lazy journalists', 3 August; <http://4thwavenow.com/2015/08/03/the-41-trans-suicide-rate-a-tale-of-flawed-data-and-lazy-journalists/>

Agius, Silvan and Christa Tobler (2011) *Trans and Intersex People: Discrimination on the Grounds of Sex, Gender Identity and Gender Expression*, European Union Publisher, European Commission. June; <http://www.refworld.org/publisher/EUCOMMISSION.html>

Ahmed, Sarah (2015) 'You are oppressing us', Feminist Killjoys. 15 February; <https://feministkilljoys.com/2015/02/15/you-are-oppressing-us/>

Anonymous Clinicians (2018) Private correspondence/interviews with Dr Heather Brunskell-Evans and Professor Michele Moore.

Anonymous Clinicians (2020) 'The Natal Female Question', Woman's Place UK. 17 February; <https://womansplaceuk.org/2020/02/17/the-natal-female-question/>

Anonymous Scientist (2016) 'A Scientist Reviews Transgender Suicide Stats', Transgender Trend. 3 December; <https://www.transgendertrend.com/a-scientist-reviews-transgender-suicide-stats/>

BAGIS (British Association of Gender Identity Specialists) (2015) 'Written evidence submitted by British Association of Gender Identity Specialists to the Transgender Equality Inquiry', Parliament Publications; <http://data.parliament.uk/writtenevidence/committeeevidence.svc/evidencedocument/women-and-equalities-committee/transgender-equality/written/19532.pdf>

Bailey, Allison (2020) 'I am suing Stonewall to stop them policing free speech', Woman's Place UK. 27 June; <https://womansplaceuk.org/2020/06/27/i-am-suing-stonewall-stop-policing-free-speech/>

Bannerman, Lucy (2017) 'Trans teenager Lily Madigan voted in as a Labour women's officer', *The Times*. 20 November; <https://www.thetimes.co.uk/article/trans-teenager-lily-madigan-voted-in-as-a-labour-women-s-officer-mwchkhzq8>

Bannerman, Lucy (2017a) 'Linda Bellos barred in Cambridge University row', *The Times*. 1 October; <https://www.thetimes.co.uk/article/linda-bellos-barred-in-cambridge-university-row-0pbdq5sm9?fbclid=IwAR2fZe-IhKi9SilBgIMtoQqrlkDjhtOcnap-ytoD4ce3hZ9g8iz4TF4dLhM>

Bannerman, Lucy (2017b) 'Barred academic Heather Brunskell-Evans warns of cowardice over trans issues', *The Times*. 23 November; <https://www.thetimes.co.uk/article/barred-academic-heather-brunskell-evans-warns-of-cowardice-over-trans-issues-wlvj3l7bz>

Bannerman, Lucy (2018) 'Cancer Research to Drop the Word Woman for Fear of Causing Offence', *The Times*. 15 June; <https://www.thetimes.co.uk/article/smear-test-campaign-drops-the-word-woman-to-avoid-transgender-offence-263mj7f6s>

Barker, Meg-John and Julia Scheele (2016) *Queer: A Graphic History*. Icon Books: London.

Barrett, James (2019) 'It's Soul Crushing and Miserable for Anyone to Live Pretending to Be Someone They Are Not', *The Friend*. 11 April; <https://thefriend.org/article/it-is-soul-crushing-and-miserable-for-anyone-to-live-pretending-to-be-somet>

BBC Newsnight (2019) 'Transgender treatment: Puberty blockers study under investigation', 22 July; <https://www.youtube.com/watch?v=1bIt5MQIozc&feature=youtu.be>

BBC Newsnight (2020) 'NHS child gender clinic: Staff welfare concerns "shut down"', 18 June; <https://www.youtube.com/watch?v=zTRnrp9pXHY&feature=youtu.be>

Bergdorf, Munroe (2018) *Twitter* @MunroeBergdorf. 20 January.

Biggs, Michael (2018) 'Suicide by trans-identified children in England and Wales', Transgender Trend; <https://www.transgendertrend.com/suicide-by-trans-identified-children-in-england-and-wales/>

Biggs, Michael (2018a) 'Attempted suicide by American LGBT adolescents', 4thWaveNow. 23 October; <https://4thwavenow.com/2018/10/23/attempted-suicide-by-american-lgbt-adolescents/>

References

Biggs, Michael (2018b) 'The Open Society Foundations and the transgender movement', 4thWaveNow. 25 May; <https://4thwavenow.com/2018/05/25/the-open-society-foundations-the-transgender-movement/>

Biggs, Michael (2018c) 'How Queer Theory Became University Policy', *Conatus News.* 24 November; <https://conatusnews.com/how-queer-theory-became-university-policy/>

Biggs, Michael (2019) 'Tavistock's Experimentation with Puberty Blockers: Scrutinizing the Evidence', Transgender Trend. 5 March; <https://www.transgendertrend.com/tavistock-experiment-puberty-blockers/>

Biggs, Michael (2019a) 'Britain's Experiment with Puberty Blockers' in Michele Moore and Heather Brunskell-Evans (eds.) (2019) *Inventing Transgender Children and Young People.* Cambridge Scholars Publishing: Newcastle upon Tyne.

Biggs, Michael (2020) 'The Transition from Sex to Gender in English Prisons: Human Rights and Queer Theory' in *SocArxiv Papers: Open Archive of the Social Sciences.* 16 May; <https://osf.io/preprints/socarxiv/43f2t/>

Bilek, Jennifer (2018) 'Who are the Rich White Men Institutionalizing Transgender Ideology?', *The Federalist.* 20 February; <https://thefederalist.com/2018/02/20/rich-white-men-institutionalizing-transgender-ideology/>

Bilek, Jennifer (2018a) 'Transgenderism is Just Big Business Dressed in Pretend Civil Rights Clothes', *The Federalist.* 5 July; <https://thefederalist.com/2018/07/05/transgenderism-just-big-business-dressed-pretend-civil-rights-clothes/>

Bilek, Jennifer (2020) 'Do Parents Have a Chance Against the Trans Lobby: Part III', *The 11th Hour.* 30 April; <https://www.the11thhourblog.com/post/do-parents-have-a-chance-against-the-trans-lobby-part-iii>

Bloody Good Period (2020) <https://www.bloodygoodperiod.com/>

Boycott-Owen, Mason (2018) 'Trans women should be considered for all-women shortlists, says Labour MP', *The Guardian.* 11 January; <https://www.theguardian.com/society/2018/jan/11/trans-women-should-be-considered-for-all-women-shortlists-labour-dawn-butler>

BPS (British Psychological Society) (2019) 'Guidelines for psychologists working with gender, sexuality and relationship diversity'; <https://www.bps.org.uk/sites/www.bps.org.uk/files/Policy/Policy%20-%20Files/Guidelines%20for%20psychologists%20working%20with%20gender%2C%20sexuality%20and%20relationship%20diversity.pdf>

Brunskell-Evans, Heather (2015) 'Neo-liberalism, Masculinity and Femininity', *Think: Leicester*. 8 June; <https://www2.le.ac.uk/offices/press/think-leicester/arts-and-culture/2015/neo-liberalism-masculinity-and-femininity-caitlyn-jenner-and-the-politics-of-transgender>

Brunskell-Evans, Heather (2017) *The Moral Maze*, BBC Radio 4. 15 November; <http://www.heather-brunskell-evans.co.uk/body-politics/moral-maze-defining-gender-bbc-radio-4/>

Brunskell-Evans, Heather (2018) 'Gendered Mis-Intelligence: The Fabrication of "The Transgender Child"' in Heather Brunskell-Evans and Michele Moore (eds.) *Transgender Children and Young People: Born in your own body*. Cambridge Scholars Publishing: Newcastle upon Tyne.

Brunskell-Evans, Heather (2018a) 'Open Letter', 6 March; <http://www.heather-brunskell-evans.co.uk/body-politics/open-letter/>

Brunskell-Evans, Heather (2019) 'The Medico-Legal "Making" of "The Transgender Child"', *Medical Law Review*, Volume 27, Issue 4, Autumn, pp. 640–657; <https://academic.oup.com/medlaw/article/27/4/640/5522968?guestAccessKey=ba15f531-f2ff-4b63-a348-2a8d58652cb9>

Brunskell-Evans, Heather (2019a) 'The Tavistock: Inventing "The Transgender Child"' in Michele Moore and Heather Brunskell-Evans (eds.) *Inventing Transgender Children and Young People*. Cambridge Scholars Publishing: Newcastle upon Tyne.

Brunskell-Evans, Heather (2019b) 'Leeds Launch of The Declaration on Women's Sex-Based Rights – Speech by Dr Heather Brunskell-Evans', 25 May; <http://www.heather-brunskell-evans.co.uk/thoughts/leeds-launch-of-the-declaration-of-womens-sex-based-rights-speech-by-dr-heather-brunskell-evans/>

Brunskell-Evans, Heather and Michele Moore (eds.) (2018) *Transgender Children and Young People: Born in your own body*. Cambridge Scholars Publishing: Newcastle upon Tyne.

Brunskell-Evans, Heather and Michele Moore (2018a) 'The Fabrication of "The Transgender Child"' in Heather Brunskell-Evans and Michele Moore (eds.) *Transgender Children and Young People: Born in your own body*. Cambridge Scholars Publishing: Newcastle upon Tyne.

Brunskell-Evans, Heather and Michele Moore (2019) 'From Born in Your Own Body to "Invention" of "the transgender child"' in Heather Brunskell-Evans and Michele Moore (eds.) *Inventing Transgender Children and Young People*. Cambridge Scholars Publishing: Newcastle upon Tyne.

Burns, Christine (ed.) (2018) *Trans Britain: Our Journey from the Shadows*. Unbound: London.

Butler, Catherine and Anna Hutchinson (2020) 'Debate: The pressing need for research and services for gender desisters/detransitioners', *Child and Adolescent Mental Health*, Volume 25, No. 1, pp. 45–47; <https://acamh.onlinelibrary.wiley.com/doi/10.1111/camh.12361>

Butler, Gary, Nastasja De Graaf, Bernadette Wren, and Polly Carmichael (2018) 'Assessment and support of children and adolescents with gender dysphoria', *Archives of Disease in Childhood*, Volume 103, No. 7, pp. 631–636; <https://adc.bmj.com/content/103/7/631>

Butler, Gary, Bernadette Wren and Polly Carmichael (2019) 'Puberty blocking in gender dysphoria: suitable for all?', *Archives of Disease in Childhood*, Volume 104, No. 6, pp. 509–510; <https://pubmed.ncbi.nlm.nih.gov/30655266/>

Butler, Judith (1990) *Gender Trouble: Feminism and the Subversion of Identity*. Routledge: New York and London.

Butler, Judith (2004) *Undoing Gender*. Routledge: New York and London.

Butler, Judith (2019) 'The backlash against "gender ideology" must stop', *The New Statesman*. January; < https://www.newstatesman.com/2019/01/judith-butler-backlash-against-gender-ideology-must-stop>

Care Quality Commission (2020) 'About Us'; <https://www.cqc.org.uk/about-us>

Carmichael, Polly (2017) 'GIDS referrals increase slows in 2016/17', Tavistock and Portman: NHS Foundation Trust; <https://tavistockandportman.nhs.uk/about-us/news/stories/gids-referrals-increase-slows-201617/>

Carmichael, Polly (2020) *Victoria Derbyshire Show*, BBC 2. Broadcast 2 March; <https://www.bbc.co.uk/iplayer/episode/m000g19g/victoria-derbyshire-02032020>

Cary, Peter (2017) 'Theresa May says "being trans is not an illness" and pledges to reform Gender Recognition Act', *The Independent*. 19 October; <https://www.independent.co.uk/news/uk/politics/theresa-may-transgender-not-illness-gender-recognition-act-lgbt-rights-sex-edution-homophobia-pink-a8008486.html>

Channel 4 (2018) *Trans Kids: It's Time to Talk*. Broadcast 21 November; <https://www.channel4.com/programmes/trans-kids-its-time-to-talk>

Cherry, Joanna (2019) 'UK Human Rights Comm. MP Joanna Cherry questions Twitter on allowing violence against women', Houses of Parliament. 3 May; <https://www.youtube.com/watch?v=S3X0LXARUTE>

Cohen, Deborah and Hannah Barnes (2019) 'Gender dysphoria in children: puberty blockers study draws further criticism', *British Medical Journal*. 20 September; <https://www.bmj.com/content/366/bmj.l5647>

Crown Prosecution Service, GOV.UK (2016) *Violence Against Women and Girls Crime Report 2015-2016*; <https://www.cps.gov.uk/sites/default/files/documents/publications/cps_vawg_report_2016.pdf>

Crown Prosecution Services, GOV.UK (2020) *Hate Crime*; <https://www.cps.gov.uk/hate-crime>

Crown Prosecution Services, GOV.UK (2020a) *Homophobic, Biphobic and Transphobic Hate Crime – Prosecution Guidance*; <https://www.cps.gov.uk/legal-guidance/homophobic-biphobic-and-transphobic-hate-crime-prosecution-guidance>

Cymbalist, Rivka (2020) 'Using Woman-Centred Language Regarding Childbirth Is About More Than Semantics', *Feminist Current*. 20 January; <https://www.feministcurrent.com/2020/01/20/using-gender-neutral-language-regarding-women-and-childbirth-is-about-more-than-semantics/>

Davies-Arai, Stephanie (2018) 'Back to school with Stonewall', Transgender Trend. 24 September; <https://www.transgendertrend.com/back-to-school-with-stonewall/>

Davies-Arai, Stephanie (2019) 'Our Statement on Stonewall', Transgender Trend. 5 July; <https://www.transgendertrend.com/our-statement-stonewall/>

Davidson, Sarah (2019) 'It's a real critical period around gender'. *The Psychologist*, September, Volume 32, pp. 46–49; <https://thepsychologist.bps.org.uk/volume-32/september-2019/its-real-critical-period-around-gender>

Derrida, Jacques (1967) *Of Grammatology*. John Hopkins University Press: Baltimore MD.

Derrida, Jacques (1973) *Speech and Phenomena and Other Essays on Husserl's Theory of Signs*. Northwestern University Press: Evanston.

Detransition Advocacy Network (2019) 'Detransition: The Elephant in the Room Part Two'; <https://www.youtube.com/watch?v=stBt7_NTT3o>

Ditum, Sarah (2018) 'Trans Rights Should Not Come at The Expense of Women's Fragile Gains', *The Economist, Open Future*. 5 July; <https://www.economist.com/open-future/2018/07/05/trans-rights-should-not-come-at-the-cost-of-womens-fragile-gains>

DOH (Department of Health) (2008) 'Medical Care for Gender Variant Children and Young People: answering families' questions', NHS England; <https://webarchive.nationalarchives.gov.uk/20130124042229/http://www.dh.gov.uk/prod_consum_dh/groups/dh_digitalassets/@dh/@en/documents/digitalasset/dh_082954.pdf>

Dowling, Aydian and Buck Angel (2019) 'Severe pain at orgasm: effect of testosterone on the female body', Transgender Trend. 18 February; <https://www.transgendertrend.com/severe-pain-orgasm-effect-testosterone-female-body/>

Endocrine Society (2017) 'Endocrine Treatment of Gender-Dysphoric/Gender-Incongruent Persons: An Endocrine Society Clinical Practice Guideline', *The Journal of Clinical Endocrinology and Metabolism* Volume 102, No. 11, pp. 3869–3903; <https://pubmed.ncbi.nlm.nih.gov/28945902/>

Entwistle, Kirsty (2019) 'An open letter to Dr Polly Carmichael from a former GIDS clinician', *Medium*. 18 July; <https://medium.com/@kirstyentwistle/an-open-letter-to-dr-polly-carmichael-from-a-former-gids-clinician-53c541276b8d>

Ettelbrick, Paula L. and Alia Trabbucco Zeran (2010) 'The Impact of the Yogyakarta Principles on International Human Rights Law Development: a study of November 2007 – June 2010', *Asia Pacific Forum of Human Rights Institutions.* November; <http://ypinaction. org/wp-content/uploads/2016/10/Yogyakarta_Principles_Impact_ Tracking_Report.pdf>

Evans, Charlie (2019) 'The medicalization of gender non-conforming children, and the vulnerability of lesbian youth', *Lesbian Strength 2019.* 16 September; <https://www.youtube.com/watch?v=-JazgA3AdUE>

Evans, Marcus (2020) 'Why I Resigned from Tavistock: Trans-Identified Children Need Therapy, Not Just "Affirmation" and Drugs', *Quillette.* 17 January; <https://quillette.com/author/marcus-evans/>

Evans, Marcus (2020a) 'Freedom to think: the need for thorough assessment and treatment of gender dysphoric children', Cambridge Core, Cambridge University Press. 21 July; <https://www.cambridge. org/core/journals/bjpsych-bulletin/article/freedom-to-think-the- need-for-thorough-assessment-and-treatment-of-gender-dysphoric- children/F4B7F5CAFC0D0BE9FF3C7886BA6E904B/core-reader>

Fair Play for Women (2017) 'Half of all transgender prisoners are sex offenders or dangerous category A inmates', 9 November; <https:// fairplayforwomen.com/transgender-prisoners/>

Fair Play for Women (2017a), 'How Often Are Transgender People Murdered?', 23 October; <https://fairplayforwomen.com/trans- murder-rates/>

Fair Play for Women (2018) 'After Karen White: What is the government doing to make sure women in prison never get attacked by a male inmate ever again?', 13 December; <https://fairplayforwomen.com/ prison-review/>

Femicide Census (2016) 'Redefining an Isolated Incident', *Femicide Census: Profiles of women killed by men.* January 2017; <https://1q7dqy2unor827bqjls0c4rn-wpengine.netdna-ssl.com/wp- content/uploads/2017/01/The-Femicide-Census-Jan-2017.pdf>

Fisher, Dan (2017) 'The Butlerian Jihad – For a New Left', *Uncommon Ground.* 7 October; <https://uncommongroundmedia.com/ countering-postmodernism-relativism/>

Finlayson, Lorna, Katharine Jenkins and Rosie Worsdale (2018) "'I'm not transphobic, but ...": A feminist case against the feminist case against trans inclusivity', *Verso*. 17 October; <https://www.versobooks.com/blogs/4090-i-m-not-transphobic-but-a-feminist-case-against-the-feminist-case-against-trans-inclusivity>

Forstater, Maya (2019) 'Has Penny Mordaunt Got Away with the Worst Mumsnet Performance Ever?', *The Independent*. 27 March; <https://www.independent.co.uk/voices/penny-mourdant-mumsnet-gender-recognition-act-a8835621.html>

Forstater, Maya (2020) 'Sex and Gender', *Hiya Maya;* <https://hiyamaya.net/sex-and-gender/>

Gender Critical Woman (2020) 'Standing up to the transcult bullies', *We Are Fair Cop*. 27 May; <https://www.faircop.org.uk/standing-up-to-the-transcult-bullies/>

Gendered Intelligence (2015) 'Written Submission to the Women and Equality Commission', Parliament Publications; <http://data.parliament.uk/writtenevidence/committeeevidence.svc/evidence document/women-and-equalities-committee/transgender-equality/written/19557.pdf>

Gendered Intelligence (2020) 'About Us: Aims and Activities'; <http://genderedintelligence.co.uk/about-us/our-aims>

Gendered Intelligence (2020a) 'Judicial Review on GIDS'; <https://genderedintelligence.wordpress.com/2020/01/06/judicial-review-on-gids/>

Gendered Intelligence (2020b) 'Professional Services'; <http://genderedintelligence.co.uk/professionals/training>

Gendered Intelligence (2020c) 'Where are we as an organisation and a movement', 3 July; <https://genderedintelligence.wordpress.com/category/gender-recognition-act/>

GIDS (Gender Identity Development Service) (2020) 'Puberty and physical intervention'; <https://gids.nhs.uk/puberty-and-physical-intervention>

GIDS (Gender Identity Development Service) (2020a) 'Referrals to GIDS, 2014-15 to 2018-19'; <https://gids.nhs.uk/number-referrals>

Gilligan, Andrew (2019) 'Staff at trans clinic fear damage to children as activists pile on pressure', *Sunday Times*. 16 February; <https://www. thetimes.co.uk/article/staff-at-trans-clinic-fear-damage-to-children-as-activists-pile-on-pressure-c5k655nq9>

GLAAD (Gay and Lesbian Alliance Against Defamation) (2015) 'GLAAD responds to Vanity Fair cover featuring Caitlyn Jenner, releases updated tip sheet for journalists', June; <https://www.glaad.org/blog/ glaad-responds-vanity-fair-cover-featuring-caitlyn-jenner-releases-updated-tip-sheet>

Goodenough, Tom (2020) 'Why are police spending thousands on Stonewall subscriptions?', *The Spectator*. 13 July; <https://www. spectator.co.uk/article/why-is-the-police-spending-money-on-stonewall-subscriptions->

Government Equalities Office (2015) 'Providing Services for Transgender Customers: A Guide', November; <https://assets.publishing.service. gov.uk/government/uploads/system/uploads/attachment_data/ file/484857/Providing_services_for_transgender_customers-a_guide. pdf.>

Government Legislation UK (2020) *Equality Act 2010*; <http://www. legislation.gov.uk/ukpga/2010/15/contents>

Government Legislation UK (2020a) *Equality Act 2010*: Section Eleven; <http://www.legislation.gov.uk/ukpga/2010/15/contents>

Government Legislation UK (2020b) *Equality Act 2010*: Section Seven; <http://www.legislation.gov.uk/ukpga/2010/15/contents>

Government Legislation UK (2020c) *Gender Recognition Act 2004*; <http://www.legislation.gov.uk/ukpga/2004/7/contents>

GOV.UK (2018) 'Reform of the *Gender Recognition Act* – Government Consultation'; <https://assets.publishing.service.gov.uk/government/ uploads/system/uploads/attachment_data/file/721725/GRA-Consultation-document.pdf>

Griffiths, Sian (2018) 'Activists thwart work on transgender law reforms', *The Sunday Times*. 28 October; <https://www.thetimes.co.uk/article/ activists-thwart-work-on-gender-law-reforms-jx6lwd6tf>

Handley, Natasha (2019) Trans Leeds; <https://www.youtube.com/ watch?v=aXYebAojtUQ>

References

Harper's Magazine (2020) 'A Letter on Justice and Open Debate', 7 July; <https://harpers.org/a-letter-on-justice-and-open-debate/>

Hawthorne, Susan (2019) *In Defence of Separatism*. Spinifex Press: Mission Beach.

Hines, Sally (2009) 'Riding the Waves: Feminism, Lesbian and Gay Politics, and the Transgender Debates' in Gurnider K. Bhambar and Ipek Demir (eds.) *1968 In Retrospect: History, Theory, Alterity*. Palgrave Macmillan: London;

Hines, Sally (2015) 'Pregnant Men: An International Exploration of Trans Male Practices of Reproduction', ESSL University of Leeds; <https://essl.leeds.ac.uk/directory_record/337/pregnant-men-an-international-exploration-of-trans-male-practices-of-reproduction>

Hines, Sally (2019) 'Pregnant Men: An International Exploration of Trans Male Experiences and Practices of Reproduction', *UK Research and Innovation*; <https://gtr.ukri.org/project/3EB70D61-77E6-46E1-9F59-47024412A921>

Hoffkling, Alexis, Juno Obedin-Maliver and Jae Sevelius (2017) 'From erasure to opportunity: a qualitative study of the experiences of transgender men around pregnancy and recommendations for providers', *BMC Pregnancy Childbirth* 17, 332; <https://bmcpregnancychildbirth.biomedcentral.com/articles/10.1186/s12884-017-1491-5>

Holt, Alison (2020) 'NHS gender clinic "should have challenged me more" over transition', BBC News Online. 1 March; <https://www.bbc.co.uk/news/health-51676020>

Home Office (2000) 'Report of The Interdepartmental Working Group On Transsexual People'; <http://www.oocities.org/transforum2000/Resources/wgtrans.pdf>

Human Rights Campaign Foundation (2020) 'Safer Sex for Trans Bodies'; <https://assets2.hrc.org/files/assets/resources/Trans_Safer_Sex_Guide_FINAL.pdf?_ga=2.198604973.305067082.1595180784-767501988.1595180784>

Human Rights Watch (2007) '"Yogyakarta Principles": A Milestone for Lesbian, Gay, Bisexual, and Transgender Right and Gender Equality', 26 March; <https://www.hrw.org/news/2007/03/26/yogyakarta-principles-milestone-lesbian-gay-bisexual-and-transgender-rights>

Human Rights Watch (2017) 'Menstrual Hygiene a Human Rights Issue: A Simple Guide to Ending Discrimination, Abuse', 27 August; <https://www.hrw.org/news/2017/08/27/menstrual-hygiene-human-rights-issue>

Hymas, Charles (2019) 'One in 50 prisoners identifies as transgender amid concerns inmates are attempting to secure prison perks', *The Telegraph.* 9 July; <https://www.telegraph.co.uk/news/2019/07/09/one-50-prisoners-identify-transsexual-first-figures-show-amid/>

Jeffreys, Sheila (2014) *Gender Hurts: A feminist analysis of the politics of transgenderism.* Routledge: London and New York.

Jones, Jane Clare (2018) 'Judith Butler: How To Disappear Patriarchy in Three Easy Steps'; <https://janeclarejones.com/2019/01/24/judith-butler-how-to-disappear-patriarchy-in-three-easy-steps/>

Jones, Jane Clare (2018a) 'The Annals of the TERF Wars'; <https://janeclarejones.com/2018/11/13/the-annals-of-the-terf-wars/>

Kay, Jonathan (2019) 'An Interview with Lisa Littman Who Coined the Term "Rapid Onset Dysphoria"', *Quillette.* 19 March; <https://quillette.com/2019/03/19/an-interview-with-lisa-littman-who-coined-the-term-rapid-onset-gender-dysphoria/>

Kennedy, Natacha and Mark Hellen (2010) 'Transgender children: more than a theoretical challenge', *Graduate Journal of Social Sciences,* December Vol.7, Issue 2; <https://www.researchgate.net/publication/50384394_Transgender_children_more_than_a_theoretical_challenge>

Labour Campaign for Trans Rights (2020) 'Founding Statement and Pledge', 10 February; <https://twitter.com/Labour_Trans>

Labour Party Manifesto (2019) <https://labour.org.uk/manifesto-2019/>

Laidlaw, Michael (2020) 'The Pediatric Endocrine Society's Statement on Puberty Blockers Isn't Just Deceptive. It's Dangerous', *Public Discourse.* 13 January; <https://www.thepublicdiscourse.com/2020/01/59422/>

Lees, Paris (2015) 'Caitlyn Jenner: a life-affirming, provocative and downright fabulous Vanity Fair cover', *The Guardian.* 2 June; <https://www.theguardian.com/tv-and-radio/2015/jun/01/caitlyn-jenner-vanity-fair-cover-life-affirming?CMP=share_btn_tw>

Letter to *Disability and Society* Editorial Board (2019) *iPetitions*; <https://www.ipetitions.com/petition/ds>

Levine, Stephen (2020) 'Expert Affidavit of Dr Stephen B. Levine, M.D. Case No. 20-CV- 454'; <http://www.will-law.org/wp-content/uploads/2020/02/affidavit-stephen-levine-with-exhibit.pdf?fbclid=I wAR0wNTBRbBoFmp3hjZhcCx2XB4s_AUb9hm5PXiRDX8L2uj25G_iQ2DombiY>

LGB Alliance (Lesbian, Gay and Bi-Sexual Alliance) (2020) <https://lgballiance.org.uk>

Littman, Lisa (2018) 'Parent reports of adolescents and young adults perceived to show signs of a rapid onset of gender dysphoria', *PLOS ONE*. 16 August; <https://journals.plos.org/plosone/article?id=10.1371/journal.pone.0202330>

Lorimer, Stuart (2017) 'GenderCare: Building a Private Trans Healthcare Service in the UK', *GENDERQUEER.ME*; <https://genderqueer.me/2017/08/10/fv-gendercare-uk/>

Ludwig, Audrey (2020) 'Legally this is not a "trans rights issue" it is a "sex rights issue" – a blog about boxes', Woman's Place UK. 2 July; <https://womansplaceuk.org/2020/07/02/legally-this-is-not-a-trans-rights-issue-its-a-sex-rights-issue-a-blog-about-boxes-audrey-ludwig/>

MANA (Midwives Alliance of North America) (2015) 'Position Statement on Gender Inclusive Language'; <https://mana.org/healthcare-policy/position-statement-on-gender-inclusive-language>

Manning, Sanchez, and Joanni Walsh (2019) 'Britain's first transgender hate crime trial is halted after one day as judge says "there is no case and never was a case"', *Daily Mail*. 2 March; <https://www.dailymail.co.uk/news/article-6764763/Britains-transgender-hate-crime-trial-halted-one-day.html>

Martian Anthropologist (2019) '"Trans" prisoners in women's prisons', 7 November; <https://herriotts.wordpress.com/2019/07/10/trans-prisoners-in-womens-prisons/>

Mermaids (2020) <https://mermaidsuk.org.uk/>

Ministry of Justice, GOV.UK (2016) 'Review on the Care and Management of Transgender Offenders', November; <https://assets.publishing.service.gov.uk/government/uploads/system/uploads/attachment_data/file/566828/transgender-review-findings-web.PDF>

Ministry of Justice, GOV.UK (2017) 'Statistics on Women and the Criminal Justice System 2017: A Ministry of Justice publication under Section 95 of the Criminal Justice Act 1991'; <https://assets.publishing.service.gov.uk/government/uploads/system/uploads/attachment_data/file/759770/women-criminal-justice-system-2017.pdf>

Ministry of Justice, GOV.UK (2020) 'The Care and Management of Individuals who are Transgender', 27 January; <https://assets.publishing.service.gov.uk/government/uploads/system/uploads/attachment_data/file/863610/transgender-pf.pdf>

Moore, Michele and Heather Brunskell-Evans (eds.) (2019) *Inventing Transgender Children and Young People*. Cambridge Scholars Publishing: Newcastle upon Tyne.

Mordaunt, Penny (2018) 'I see a chamber filled with powerful and strong women', House of Commons, GOV.UK; <https://www.gov.uk/government/speeches/penny-mordaunt-i-see-a-chamber-filled-with-powerful-and-strong-women>

Mordaunt, Penny (2019) 'Speech: Minister for Women and Equalities Penny Mordaunt: Stonewall Workplace Conference London 2019', GOV.UK; <https://www.gov.uk/government/speeches/minister-for-women-and-equalities-penny-mordaunt-stonewall-workplace-conference-london-2019>

Murphy, Meghan (2016) 'Are We Women or Are We Menstruators?', *Feminist Current*. 7 September; <https://www.feministcurrent.com/2016/09/07/are-we-women-or-are-we-menstruators/>

Murray, Kath and Lucy Hunter Blackburn (2019) 'Losing sight of women's rights: The unregulated introduction of gender self-identification as a case study of policy capture in Scotland', *Scottish Affairs*, Volume 28, No. 3, pp. 262–289; <https://www.euppublishing.com/doi/abs/10.3366/scot.2019.0284>

Murray, Kath, Lucy Hunter Blackburn and Lisa Mackenzie (2020) 'Census (Amendment) (Scotland) Bill: data user views', MBM Policy Analysis; <https://murrayblackburnmackenzie.org/census-amendment-scotland-bill-data-user-views/>

Nandy, Lisa (2020) 'Lisa Nandy says child rapists should be in women's prisons'; <https://www.youtube.com/watch?v=lcULPSew2kU>

Nandy, Lisa (2020a) *Today Programme,* BBC Radio Four. 13 February; <https://womansplaceuk.org/wp-content/uploads/2020/02/Lisa-Nandy-TranscriptToday13.2.20.pdf>

Necati, Yas (2018) 'Without Your Rights I can't have My Rights: Dawn Butler on the importance of intersectionality at the UK's first transgender conference', *The Independent.* 12 September; <https://www.independent.co.uk/news/uk/home-news/dawn-butler-transgender-uk-labour-intersectionality-rights-a8534761.html>

NHS England (2015) 'NHS Standard Contract for Gender Identity Development Service for Children and Adolescents'; <https://www.england.nhs.uk/wp-content/uploads/2017/04/gender-development-service-children-adolescents.pdf>

Oldereide, Andrea (2020) 'The LGB Alliance's controversial views on trans-rights', *Outnews Global.* 25 January; <http://outnewsglobal.com/the-lgb-alliances-controversial-views-on-trans-rights/>

O'Malley, Stella (2019) 'Trans Kids: It's Time to Talk' in Michele Moore and Heather Brunskell-Evans (eds.) *Inventing Transgender Children and Young People.* Cambridge Scholars Publishing: Newcastle upon Tyne.

ONS (Office for National Statistics), GOV.UK (2020) 'Table 26 – Homicides by Age and Sex for England and Wales, year ending March 2019'; <https://www.ons.gov.uk/peoplepopulationandcommunity/crimeandjustice/datasets/appendixtableshomicideinenglandandwales>

Open Society Foundations *(2020) 'Our History';* <https://www.opensocietyfoundations.org/who-we-are/our-history>

Paton, Stephen (2019) 'Nicola Sturgeon: Trans rights are not a threat to me as a woman or to my feminism', *The National Newspaper.* 7 February; <https://www.thenational.scot/news/17416732.nicola-sturgeon-trans-rights-are-not-a-threat-to-me-as-a-woman-or-to-my-feminism/>

Peak Trans (2019) 'Hate from Transactivists'; <https://www.peaktrans.org/hate-from-trans-activists/>

Peak Trans (2020) 'Trying to Stop Us from Meeting'; <https://www.peaktrans.org/trying-to-stop-us-meeting/>

Petter, Olivia (2017) 'Topshop Removes Women-Only Changing Rooms', *Independent*. 8 November; <https://www.independent.co.uk/life-style/fashion/topshop-removes-women-only-changing-rooms-shops-policy-single-sex-high-street-gender-neutral-a8043771.html>

Phipps, Alison (2020) *Me Not You: The Trouble with Mainstream Feminism*. Manchester University Press: Manchester.

PinkNews (2020) 'About Us'; <https://www.pinknews.co.uk/about-us/>

Powell, Gary (2020) 'Local authorities should stop funding Stonewall', *Conservative Home*. 16 June; <https://www.conservativehome.com/localgovernment/2020/06/gary-powell-local-authorities-should-stop-funding-stonewall.html>

Public Health England, GOV.UK (2020) 'Ensuring Pregnant Trans Men Get Equal Quality Care', 13 March; <https://phescreening.blog.gov.uk/2020/03/13/pregnant-men-best-care/>

Raymond, Janice (1980) *The Transsexual Empire*. The Women's Press: London.

Robbins, Jane (2019) 'The Cracks in the Edifice of Transgender Totalitarianism', *Public Discourse*. 13 July; <https://www.thepublicdiscourse.com/2019/07/54272/>

Ross, Alex (2018) 'Protesters filmed interrupting talk on transgender issues at University of Bristol', *Bristol Post*. 22 November; <https://www.bristolpost.co.uk/news/bristol-news/protesters-filmed-interrupting-talk-transgender-2247064>

Rowling, Joanne K. (2020) 'J.K. Rowling Writes about Her Reasons for Speaking out on Sex and Gender Issues', 26 June; <https://www.jkrowling.com/opinions/j-k-rowling-writes-about-her-reasons-for-speaking-out-on-sex-and-gender-issues/>

Rowling, Joanne K. (2020a) in Harriet Brewis (2020) 'JK Rowling says she has received thousands of messages thanking her for 'speaking up' amid trans row', *Evening Standard*. 31 June; <https://www.standard.co.uk/showbiz/celebrity-news/jk-rowling-3000-messages-trans-row-domestic-abuse-a4482486.html>

Rubin, Gayle (1982) 'Thinking Sex: Notes for a Radical Theory of the Politics of Sexuality' in Carol Vance (ed) (1982) *Pleasure and Danger: Exploring Female Sexuality*. Routledge and Kegan Paul: Boston, London, Melbourne and Henley.

References

Scottish Government (2017) 'Review of the GRA: A Consultation'; <https://consult.gov.scot/family-law/review-of-the-gender-recognition-act-2004/supporting_documents/SCT10172517581_Gender_p4%203.pdf>

Screenshots (2020) 'J. K. Rowling and the trans activists: a story in screen shots', *Medium*. 9 June; <https://medium.com/@rebeccarc/j-k-rowling-and-the-trans-activists-a-story-in-screenshots-78e01dca68d>

Shriers, Abigail (2020) *Irreversible Damage: The Transgender Craze Seducing Our Daughters*. Regnery Publishing: Washington D.C.

SEGM (Society for Evidence Based Gender Medicine) (2020); <https://www.segm.org>

Sex Discrimination Act 1975 (repealed) (2020) Legislation, GOV.UK; <http://www.legislation.gov.uk/ukpga/1975/65>

Sky News (2018) 'Woman billboard was "transphobic" and "dangerous"', 26 September; <https://www.youtube.com/watch?v=y8nViKYmEhU>

Smith, Karen Ingala (2017) 'Counting Dead Women'; <https://kareningalasmith.com/counting-dead-women/>

Spiked Online (2020) 'Trans rapists do not belong in women's prisons', 17 February; <https://www.spiked-online.com/2020/02/17/trans-rapists-do-not-belong-in-womens-prisons/>

Steel, Helen (2017) 'Statement on events at Anarchist Bookfair 2017'; <https://helensteelbookfairstatement.wordpress.com>

Steel, Helen (2018) 'Helen Steel Speaking at "A Woman's Place Is on The Platform" Cambridge UK 23 November 2017', February; <https://gendercriticalgreens.wordpress.com/2018/02/17/helen-steel-speaking-at-a-womans-place-is-on-the-platform-cambridge-uk-23rd-november-2017/>

Stewart, Jay (2015) 'We Are Living on the Cusp of a Gender Revolution'; <https://www.youtube.com/watch?v=UpQd-VrKgFI >

Stewart, Jay (2018) 'Frequently asked questions about children's gender identity and expression', *Journal of Child Psychotherapy*, Volume 44, No. 1, pp. 47–54; <https://www.tandfonline.com/doi/abs/10.1080/0075417X.2018.1446455>

Stock, Kathleen (2019) 'Ignoring Differences Between Men and Women Is the Wrong Way to Address Gender Dysphoria', *Quillette*. 11 April; <https://quillette.com/2019/04/11/ignoring-differences-between-men-and-women-is-the-wrong-way-to-address-gender-dysphoria/>

Stonewall (2015) 'Written evidence submitted by Stonewall to the Transgender Equality Inquiry', 2 August; <http://data.parliament.uk/writtenevidence/committeeevidence.svc/evidencedocument/women-and-equalities-committee/transgender-equality/written/20371.pdf>

Stonewall (2018) 'Speaker's House Event Highlights Urgency of Trans Equality', 15 May; <https://www.stonewall.org.uk/about-us/media-centre/media-statement/speaker%E2%80%99s-house-event-highlights-urgency-trans-equality>

Stonewall (2019) 'Creating a trans-inclusive school environment – response to Transgender Trend', 14 Feb; <https://www.stonewall.org.uk/node/62946.>

Stonewall (2020) 'Glossary of Terms'; <https://www.stonewall.org.uk/help-advice/glossary-terms#trans>.

Stonewall (2020a) 'Trans Women Are Women. Get Over It! t-shirt'; <https://stonewalluk.myshopify.com/products/trans-women-are-women-get-over-it-t-shirt>

Stonewall (2020b) 'Grant Funding'; <https://www.stonewall.org.uk/get-involved/get-involved-fundraise-us/grant-funding>

Stonewall (2020c) 'Our Children and Young Peoples Services Champions Members'; <https://www.stonewall.org.uk/cypschampions>

Stonewall (2020d) 'Children and Young People's Services Champions programme'; <https://www.stonewall.org.uk/children-and-young-peoples-services-champions-programme#trainingsupport>

Stonewall (2020e) 'Consultancy services for education and youth professionals'; <https://www.stonewall.org.uk/consultancy-services-education-and-youth-professionals>

Sullivan, Alice (2020) 'Sex and the census: why surveys should not conflate sex and gender identity', *International Journal of Social Research Methodology 2020*, Volume 23, No. 5, 517–524; <https://www.tandfonline.com/doi/full/10.1080/13645579.2020.1768346>

They Say This Never Happens (2020) <https://theysaythisneverhappens. tumblr.com>

Trans Crime UK (2017) 'Trans Homicides in the UK: A Closer Look at the Numbers', 16 November; <http://transcrimeuk.com/2017/11/16/trans-homicides-in-the-uk-a-closer-look-at-the-numbers/>

Trans Crime UK (2018) 'Karen White', 17 July; <http://transcrimeuk. com/2018/07/17/karen-white/>

Trans Crime UK (2020) <http://transcrimeuk.com/>

Transgender Trend (2019) 'Suicide Facts and Myths'; <https://www. transgendertrend.com/the-suicide-myth/>

Transgender Trend (2020) 'BBC Newsnight report on the Tavistock GIDS', 20 June; <https://www.transgendertrend.com/bbc-newsnight-tavistock-gids/>

Transgender Trend (2020a) 'Launch of our RSE Guide for Schools', 25 June; <https://www.transgendertrend.com/launch-rse-guide-schools/>

Trans Respect Rather Than Transphobia Worldwide (2017) 'Trans Murder Monitoring. 2017', November; <https://transrespect.org/wpcontent/uploads/2017/11/TvT_TMM_TDoR2017_SimpleTable_EN.pdf>

Truss, Elizabeth (2020) 'Minister for Women and Equalities Liz Truss sets out priorities to Women and Equalities Select Committee', GOV.UK. 22 April; <https://www.gov.uk/government/speeches/minister-for-women-and-equalities-liz-truss-sets-out-priorities-to-women-and-equalities-select-committee>

Turner, Camilla (2020) 'University cancelled seminar by feminist following threats of protest by transactivists', *The Telegraph*. 17 January; <https://www.telegraph.co.uk/news/2020/01/17/university-cancelled-seminar-feminist-speaker-following-threats/>

Turner, Camilla (2020a) 'Oxford college investigates after female lecturer is "no platformed" at feminist summit', *The Telegraph*. 3 March; <https://www.telegraph.co.uk/news/2020/03/03/oxford-college-investigates-feminist-lecturer-barred-womens/>

Turner, Janice (2017) 'The battle over gender has turned bloody', *The Times*. 16 September; <https://www.thetimes.co.uk/article/the-battle-over-gender-has-turned-bloody-2wpkmnqhh>

Turner, Janice (2018) 'Even a party for women won't take on the trans lobby', *The Times*. 1 March; <https://www.thetimes.co.uk/article/even-a-party-for-women-won-t-take-on-trans-lobby-hncf8ljnn>

Turner, Janice (2020) 'Giving Puberty Blockers to "Trans" Children is a Leap into the Dark', *Sunday Times*. February 21; <https://www.thetimes.co.uk/article/giving-puberty-blocker-to-trans-children-is-a-leap-into-the-unknown-x3g37sb7f >

Turner, Janice (2020a) 'The righteous anger train is out of control', *The Times*. 27 June; <https://www.thetimes.co.uk/article/the-righteous-anger-train-is-out-of-control-0zq3cgdkk>

Two Hare Court Chambers (2018) 'Gudrun Young successfully defends leading feminist anti-racist campaigner Linda Bellos', 30 November; <https://www.2harecourt.com/2018/11/30/gudrun-young-successfully-defends-leading-feminist-anti-racist-campaigner-linda-bellos-obe/>

UKCP (UK Council for Psychotherapy) (2017) 'Memorandum of Understanding'; <https://www.psychotherapy.org.uk/wp-content/uploads/2018/07/UKCP-Memorandum-of-Understanding-2-on-Conversion-Therapy-in-the-UK.pdf>

UKCP (UK Council for Psychotherapy) (2018) 'UKCP joins leading bodies to unite against conversion therapy'; <https://www.psychotherapy.org.uk/news/ukcp-joins-leading-bodies-to-unite-against-conversion-therapy/>

UK Research and Innovation (2019) 'Pregnant Men: An International Exploration of Trans Male Experiences and Practices of Reproduction'; <https://gtr.ukri.org/projects?ref=ES%2FN019067%2F1>

Van Horn, Elizabeth (2019) 'Going back: The people reversing their gender transition', BBC Radio 4: File on Four. 26 November; <https://www.bbc.co.uk/programmes/m000bmy9>

Van Meter, Quentin (2018) 'The terrible fraud of "transgender medicine"', January 14; <https://www.youtube.com/watch?v=6mtQ1geeD_c >

Ward, Victoria (2018) 'Radical feminist warned to refer to transgender defendant as "she" during assault case', *The Telegraph*. 12 April; <https://www.telegraph.co.uk/news/2018/04/12/radical-feminist-warned-refer-transgender-defendant-assault/>

Waugh, Paul (2018) 'Labour Confirms Self-Identifying Trans Women Eligible for All-Women Shortlists And Women's Officer Roles', *Huffington Post;* <https://www.huffingtonpost.co.uk/entry/labour-confirms-self-identifying-trans-women-eligible-for-all-women-shortlists-and-womens-officer-roles_uk_5b048276e4b0784cd2af3d32?guccounter=1>

Whelan, Ella (2017) 'Lily Madigan is not a woman', *Spiked Online.* 22 November; <https://www.spiked-online.com/2017/11/22/lily-madigan-is-not-a-woman/>

Williams, Zoe (2020) 'Feminist solidarity empowers everyone. The movement must be trans-inclusive', *The Guardian.* 10 March; <https://www.theguardian.com/society/2020/mar/10/feminist-solidarity-empowers-everyone-the-movement-must-be-trans-inclusive>

Women and Equalities Committee, GOV.UK (2016) 'Transgender Equality First Report of Session 2015–16', House of Commons. Parliament Publications; <https://publications.parliament.uk/pa/cm201516/cmselect/cmwomeq/390/390.pdf>

Woman-Centered Midwifery (2015) 'Open Letter To MANA', 20 August; <https://womancenteredmidwifery.wordpress.com/take-action/>

Women's Declaration (2019) 'Declaration on Women's Sex-based Rights', Women's Human Rights Campaign; <https://womensdeclaration.com/en/resources/>

WPATH (World Professional Association of Transgender Health) (2011) 'Standards of Care for the Health of Transgender, Transsexual and Gender Non-conforming People', 7th Version; <www.wpath.org>

WPATH (World Professional Association of Transgender Health) (2020) 'History of the Association'; <https://www.wpath.org/about/history>

WPUK (Woman's Place UK) (2017) 'Making Sure a Woman's Place is on the Platform', 28 November; <https://womansplaceuk.org/making-sure-a-womans-place-is-on-the-platform/>

WPUK (Woman's Place UK) (2018) 'Linda Bellos: Self-defence is no offence'; <https://womansplaceuk.org/linda-bellos-self-defence-is-no-offence/>

WPUK (Woman's Place UK) (2019) 'About a WPUK'; <https://womansplaceuk.org/about/>

WPUK (Woman's Place UK) (2019a) 'WPUK Manifesto 2019', 20 May; <https://womansplaceuk.org/wpuk-manifesto-2019/>

WPUK (Woman's Place UK) (2019b) 'A Woman's Place is at a Conference', 26 September; <https://womansplaceuk.org/2019/09/26/a-womans-place-is-at-conference/>

WPUK (Woman's Place UK) (2020) 'A Record of Woman's Place UK Meetings'; <https://womansplaceuk.org/a-record-of-womans-place-uk-meetings/>

WPUK (Woman's Place UK) (2020a) 'No answer from Labour over intimidation', 15 February; <https://womansplaceuk.org/2020/02/15/no-answer-from-labour-over-intimidation/>

WPUK (Woman's Place UK) (2020b) 'Dear Keir', 5 April; <https://womansplaceuk.org/2020/04/05/dear-keir/>

Wren, Bernadette (2014) 'Thinking postmodern and practising in the enlightenment: Managing uncertainty in the treatment of children and adolescents', *Feminism and Psychology*, Volume 24, No. 2, pp. 271–291; <https://journals.sagepub.com/doi/full/10.1177/0959353514526223>

Wren, Bernadette (2020) 'You can't take politics out of the debate on gender diverse children', *Child and Adolescent Mental Health*, Volume 25, No. 1, pp. 40–42; <https://acamh.onlinelibrary.wiley.com/doi/full/10.1111/camh.12350>

Wright, Colin M. and Emma N. Hilton (2020) 'The Dangerous Denial of Sex', *WSJ: Opinion*. 13 February; <https://www.wsj.com/articles/the-dangerous-denial-of-sex-11581638089>

Yeomans, Emma (2019) 'Journal editors quit in protest over "transphobic" academic', *The Times*. 26 June; <https://www.thetimes.co.uk/article/journal-editors-quit-in-protest-over-transphobic-academic-6tvq3cwfv>

Yogyakarta Principles (2007) 'Introduction'; <https://yogyakartaprinciples.org/introduction/>

YouTube (2018): 'Julie Bindel confronts trans MRAs at the We Need To Talk About Sex (#weneedtotalk) event'; <https://www.youtube.com/watch?v=sBll45tSKzc>

Acknowledgements

In 2017, a grassroots movement sprang up in the UK. In those early days we felt like David facing the mighty power of Goliath. I want to thank those individuals and organisations who gave me succour, support and strength at that time (even if they didn't know it) when I was petrified of speaking but did it anyway. They too spoke out against a background of threats and intimidation. We were without institutional backing and some of us were deeply worried about the possibility of losing our jobs. We were armed only with our critical faculties, our sense of injustice, the impulse to speak truth to power and, despite some differences of opinion, a growing sense of solidarity in resistance.

A Woman's Place UK was particularly important to me and I thank Judith Green, Kiri Tunks and Ruth Serwotka for giving me a platform in 2017 when I was still shell-shocked from entering the trans ideological fray.

Stephanie Davies-Arai of Transgender Trend was a *tour de force* at that time, almost single-handedly taking on the fight to protect children.

Nicola Williams started Fair Play for Women, valiantly drawing attention to the consequences for women's prisons and sports when the 'right' of 'transwomen' to occupy those spaces was endorsed by government and human rights organisations.

I would like to thank Venice Allan, organiser of Let A Woman Speak, and Kellie-Jay Keen (aka Posie Parker), organiser of We Need to Talk, for refusing to be silenced and for injecting some irreverent fun into the first steps of our joint journey.

Hannah Clarke of Man Friday declared the trans movement the latest 'war on women', using rousing words which at that time I hardly dared speak myself.

Gender critical feminists on Mumsnet immediately came on board to support and amplify my voice. A small group of journalists began to give oxygen to our views, in particular *The Times* and *Sunday Times* journalist Janice Turner, recent winner of the 2020 Orwell Prize for Journalism.

A small supportive friendship group grew out of our joint cause: Stephanie Davies-Arai, Elin Lewis (pseudonym), Susan Matthews, Lily Maynard, Michele Moore and a friend who needs to remain anonymous. I could message women at midnight or even later when one or other was usually still awake writing or blogging. I give particular thanks to Michele Moore who, sharing crisps and wine at the end of our working day, never forgot to inject humanity and vision into our late night conversations.

Julian Vigo sustained me over the airwaves from different European countries with her fierce intelligence and intense unabashed indignation at the lack of intellectual rigour of queer theory proponents.

James Caspian, whilst walking our dogs, drew me into conversations about Jung and the current slavish deference to the new 'truth' as the latest example of the Collective Unconscious. It was comforting to hear an alternative view of the madness.

Finally, I thank my family and friends for whom my feminist activity in the past three years has not come as a surprise and who have unstintingly and unequivocally stood by me. My sons are horrified about the erosion of women's rights to single-sex safe spaces and the attempt to muzzle their mother and other women. My daughter, the criminal barrister Gudrun Young, has defended gender critical individuals against criminalisation for exercising the right to free speech.

In a cultural climate where publishing companies are shamefully risk averse to publishing anything which does not affirm the 'gender identity' orthodoxy, I would also like to give my heartfelt thanks to Spinifex Press for inviting me to write this book.

*If you would like to know more about Spinifex Press,
write to us for a free catalogue, visit our website
or email us for further information.*
Spinifex Press
PO Box 105
Mission Beach QLD 4852
Australia
www.spinifexpress.com.au
women@spinifexpress.com.au